Strikes in Europe
and the United States

Strikes in Europe and the United States

Measurement and Incidence

Kenneth Walsh

St. Martin's Press, New York

Library of Congress Card Catalog Number: 83–40055

ISBN 0-312-76641-6

ȝ 7-5-86

To Deborah

CONTENTS

LIST OF TABLES

LIST OF FIGURES

ABBREVIATIONS

ACAS	Advisory, Conciliation and Arbitration Service (UK)
AFL-CIO	American Federation of Labor – Confederation of Industrial Organisations
BLS	Bureau of Labor Statistics (USA)
CBI	Confederation of British Industry
CBS	Centraal Bureau voor de Statistiek (Netherlands)
CNPF	French Confederation of Employers
CSO	Central Statistics Office (Ireland)
DE	Department of Employment (UK)
DGB	German Trade Union Confederation
DS	Danish Statistical Office
EC	European Commission
EEC	European Economic Community
FGTB	Belgian Confederation of Labour
FRG	Federal Republic of Germany
ICTU	Irish Congress of Trade Unions
ILO	International Labour Office
INS	Belgian National Statistical Office
ISIC	International Standard Industrial Classifications
ISTAT	Italian National Statistical Agency
LO	Danish Confederation of Trade Unions
MLH	Minimum List Headings (UK)
NACE	Classification of Economic Activities in the European Communities
OECD	Organisation for Economic Co-operation and Development
SIC	Standard Industrial Classification (UK)
SOEC	Statistical Office of the European Communities
TUC	Trades Union Congress (UK)
UBO	Unemployment Benefit Office (UK)
VBO	Union of Belgian Enterprises
VNO	Federation of Netherlands industry

PREFACE

This book is primarily intended as a reference book for those using and more generally interested in the measurement of work stoppages internationally. The nine countries covered—Belgium, Denmark, France, the Federal Republic of Germany, Ireland, Italy, the Netherlands, the UK and the USA—have all collected such statistics for a long period of time and are frequently used in comparisons.

The main impetus for the book was an interest both in the subject of stoppages as one aspect of labour market information and in that of the general area of industrial relations, both engendered by my work at the Institute of Manpower Studies. Statistics on strikes, in particular, are frequently used as a proxy measure for the general tone of industrial relations in many countries and because of this, it is important that the limitations of the data are understood by the user, otherwise spurious conclusions could result.

A section of the book is also devoted to an analysis of the basic data over a ten-year period from 1972 to 1981 and, as such, represents the most complete source of statistics on stoppages recently available for the nine countries. The intention is that this data should be couched in terms of the limitations of the statistics presented in the first part of the book, and so those readers attracted more to the statistical comparisons in Part III are encouraged as a preliminary to read the discussion in Part I.

The book was made possible only with the initial stimulus provided by work originally commissioned by the Statistical Office of the European Communities on member countries, and particular thanks are due to David Harris, Director, Social and Economic Statistics, in connection with this project. Also, the individual national chapters have been put together with the assistance of staff interviewed in the relevant organisations in each country and so thanks are extended to the following bodies: Institut National du Statistique, Brussels; Danmarks Statistik, Copenhagen; Ministère du Travail (Divison de la Statistique), Paris; Statistisches Bundesamt, Weisbaden; Central Statistics Office, Dublin; Istituto Centrale di Statistica, Rome; Centraal Bureau voor de Statistiek, Voorburg; Department of Employment, London; and the US Bureau of Labor Statistics, Washington DC. All organisations have given permission for their statistics to be reproduced and this is gratefully acknowledged (in the case of the UK permission has come from the Controller of Her Majesty's Stationery Office). The form on pp. 46–7 is reproduced by permission of the Irish Central Statistics Office.

Thanks must also go to the Institute of Manpower Studies which has provided both time and facilities to complete the work and to my colleagues for their help and encouragement. The daunting task of producing the manuscript and its many tables was carried out with exemplary good humour and finesse by Dorothy Berry-Lound, with grateful thanks from the author.

Kenneth Walsh   February 1983
Institute of Manpower Studies
University of Sussex
Brighton
England

PART I

INTERNATIONAL COMPARISONS

1 INTRODUCTION

At the beginning of any book concerned with the analysis of industrial disputes or a particular type of industrial action, it is important to clarify the terminology used and to outline the common interpretations of such terminology. In works which are concentrating on international comparisons as well, then it is even more important to do so. It should not be surprising, therefore, that the first part of this introductory chapter is devoted to a discussion of the term 'industrial dispute' and its relationship to the forms of action that frequently arise during the course of a dispute.

Generally, the term 'industrial dispute' is applied to a situation where there is disagreement between workers and management (the employer) over a particular issue or issues. This, however, is defining the term somewhat crudely for the sake of clarity, since such a dispute could arise because of friction between two trade unions, for example, where management, in so far as the immediate cause of the dispute is concerned, may have only a peripheral involvement. In other cases, it could start from some wider cause beyond straightforward employer–employee relationships, perhaps over some political protest issue, though it must be said that even in cases such as these, most disputes with a so-called *political* motive have their origins in some wider-based industrial issue.

In some ways the term 'industrial' can be misleading in itself. This should not be interpreted as an indication that disputes only apply to the traditional concept of industry, the primary and manufacturing sectors of industry. In discussing industrial disputes it should be clear that all sectors of industry and services may be affected, though, as will be revealed in subsequent chapters, some of the countries covered in this study do exclude certain sectors and groups of workers from taking part in strikes, for example, which effectively excludes those sectors from the statistics. Such cases may be considered the exception, however, and most countries do not have large-scale exclusions of either industries or occupations.

Forms of industrial action

So the term 'industrial dispute' is in many respects a broad definition, which can manifest itself in a variety of different forms of action which take place within the employing organisation. Such action includes the strike or its corollary the lockout, as well as go-slows, work-to-rules, non-co-operative measures, overtime bans or higher than usual levels of absenteeism. These are the main forms of action usually to be found, but there are others and some will be peculiar to a particular organisation or industry. Similarly some types of action are more effective than others in certain occupations. Clearly, for example, an overtime ban will be an effective measure to take only where loss of overtime working will seriously affect the normal work, as in the case of most public transport.

It should also be remembered that not all of the forms of industrial action listed (as well as those not listed) operate independently. In some instances there will be a series of measures being taken simultaneously or even consecutively in an ordered programme of measures starting from the potentially least damaging to the most damaging. It is a well established procedure for workers to bring pressure on management by introducing a series of measures which get progressively worse as deliberations become more drawn out. However there is little statistical evidence available to enable an assessment of the relative efficacy of the different types of action to be made.

It has also been argued that many of the possible forms of industrial action are used interchangeably as circumstances dictate, such that one will be substituted for another or more different measures.[1] This typically arises in the cases where strike action is suppressed for one reason or another. The reasons for the suppression can be blatant, such as in the case of laws which prohibit strike action during the currency of a collective agreement (common in many of the countries covered in this study), or more covert, for example where external labour market conditions (as, say, proxied by high levels of unemployment) dissuade workers from striking. In such situations it may be considered more appropriate to take another form of action in place of striking to show the extent of unrest and to bring pressure to bear on the employer in the same way.

Recent research in the UK has provided some idea of the degree of this interchangeability between the different forms of industrial action. Brown reports that from evidence gathered in a workplace survey carried out in 1977–8, overtime bans were reported in 69 per cent of those establishments reporting some strike action over a two-year period, and 37 per cent reported a work-to-rule.[2] It is difficult to be clear about the degree of substitutability between such measures from the available data, but in comparing the results of this survey with another workplace survey carried out in the UK in 1972,[3] it would seem that the percentage of establishments which experienced a strike and some other form of industrial action over the review period was higher then than in 1977-8. In other words, over the five-year period in the UK the incidence of other forms of action has moved in the same direction as that for strikes, which tends to indicate that the relationship is complementary rather than one of substitutability.

However, the problem is that though it is acknowledged that the other forms of action do occur probably in significant quantities in all the nine countries covered in this study, apart from the occasional workplace survey carried out in a few of them, only a small number of these types of action are systematically measured. This is partly a reflection of the difficulties of, firstly, defining and, secondly, measuring such apparently obscure forms of action as a work-to-rule, for example. Therefore, of the most common types of action taken only three are measured regularly, and these are strikes, lockouts and absenteeism, but all three are collected in only a few of the countries.

Of these three measures, absenteeism is the least consistent and most problematic with only some of the countries covered in this study attempting to assess its scale. But in such cases, the data is usually confined to that absence from work caused by illness, which has been certificated under national procedures and so can be counted from social insurance records. Clearly such types of absence are not relevant to any analysis of industrial disputes where the useful information should relate to voluntary or casual absence, in other words, absence which has been taken by the worker either in protest or in response to dissatisfaction with conditions at work. In these terms, the limited information on absence regularly collected and published by some of the countries is virtually useless as an indicator of industrial unrest, leaving strikes and lockouts as the only two types of action that are regularly measured in all the countries covered in this study and that directly relate to industrial unrest.

Strikes and lockouts

Frequently strikes and lockouts are collectively called 'stoppages of work' in much of the literature and in this study the terms are used interchangeably. Similarly, it should be made clear that the term 'industrial dispute' is often used to mean a strike and so can also be considered interchangeable with the other two expressions.

Of strikes and lockouts, it is the strike which represents the most prominent type of action. However, both forms of action are well defined by the International Labour Office (ILO) definition of an industrial dispute which goes as follows:

a temporary stoppage of work wilfully effected by a group of workers or by one or more employers with a view to enforcing a demand . . .[4]

The strike component is only the action effected by the workers and the lockout identifies the employer or group of employers as the chief protagonist. Emphasis is placed on the words 'temporary' and 'wilfully' in this definition in an effort to show that strikes involve the *voluntary* withdrawal of labour and lockouts the *voluntary* shutting out of the workforce, in both cases as a *temporary* interruption to normal working practices. The subsequent pages show that there are significant differences in the toleration of stoppages of work in the countries covered, some limiting strike action and others curtailing lockouts. In all cases, however, there is some attempt to measure both within the confines of the broader definition given by the ILO and within the limits of the national laws and conventions in the general conduct of industrial relations.

The format followed

This book is concerned fundamentally with providing a work of reference on the comparative measurement of stoppages of work in the eight European Community (EC) countries of Belgium, Denmark, France, the Federal Republic of Germany, Ireland, Italy, the Netherlands and the United Kingdom (UK), and outside the EC the USA is brought in to widen the perspective. The assessment of comparability is achieved through a thorough understanding of the method of measurement used in each country and the inherent problems in those methods, with such findings reported individually in Part II.

Part III of the book uses the available statistics from each country to provide a comparative assessment of the trend of stoppage activity over the period 1972–81 (where the available statistics permit), with particular emphasis on the classification of the data by cause, duration, and industry groups, representing the main dimensions of activity. There is also a full discussion of the relative trade union and industrial relations structures to be found in each country (Chapter 16) in an attempt to show the differences that exist in these important factors, which will aid a fuller understanding of the different stoppage trends displayed in each country.

International comparisons

The reasons for comparing statistics of stoppages of work internationally are for the most part ingrained in the desire to know what the position of one country is relative to another. It not only applies to stoppages, but is to be found in all manner of economic and labour market indicators, as well as in the more hackneyed comparisons of the so-called measures of the standard of living such as the ownership of telephones, cars, or freezers. On such a level, international comparisons are mainly used to establish league tables of countries based on their relative position in the measure or combination of measures used.

However, even on such an apparently superficial level it is important that the statistics used in such comparisons are the best available and that where inconsistencies do exist, then these are pointed out for the benefit of the uninitiated reader. It is commonly the case that outsiders' perceptions of some particular countries are based on nothing more than spurious statistical comparisons of incompatible data. It can do a great deal of damage to the reputation a country has or is permitted to have in the eyes of such outsiders. But if this problem of data comparisons was confined to overall impressions of a country, that would be damaging enough. However, the fact is that certain key aspects of economic and manpower information are crucial to the well-being of certain countries within the international community. This is nowhere more apparent than in the broad field of industrial relations.

The decision of a multinational company to invest in new plant in a new location characterises the problem. Typically the company will be looking for a site to establish a base within a potentially lucrative market and will be faced in most cases with a choice of possible locations, the final one of which will be chosen on the basis of a thorough appraisal of the major economic factors appropriate to the investing company. Certainly amongst these will be consideration of sites available, grants and loans for development, transport facilities and related factors. Also to be considered, however, will be the manpower side, and for some industries more than others the record of industrial relations in specific locations will be of prime importance.

The comparison problem becomes more acute for member countries of a unified customs zone such as the European Community. Theoretically, the prospective investing company will be faced with an array of possible locations across the member countries, each one vying for priority, with each keen to promote the comparative benefits of their particular area. The problem has become more intense with high levels of unemployment affecting all EC countries. This has resulted in not only inter-country rivalry, but also competition within countries as each individual site tries to win the development, as illustrated in the UK in 1981 in the case of the Japanese Nissan motor car plant, where competition reached fever pitch before the project was shelved in 1982.[5] Here, given the particular industry and the previous record of comparatively turbulent industrial relations, the individual industrial relations records of the short-listed sites were a key factor in the ultimate decision.[6]

The problem is that if, as is frequently the case in the absence of other accessible data, strikes are used as a proxy for the general record of industrial relations and national statistics are compared internationally, then this will probably lead to erroneous results. The measurement of strikes in the nine countries covered in this study in most cases differs sufficiently to throw serious doubt on the validity of international comparisons. As will be shown, no two countries can really be said to be compiling their strike statistics on the same basis, though some are obviously closer than others. The inclusion of the USA in the study is particularly appropriate in this case, since that country has provided the mainstay of foreign-owned investment in the EC countries. As such it is inevitable that US multi-nationals will draw comparisons between industrial relations at home and those in Europe, though it must be said (and this will be discussed more fully in Part III), that most European countries compare favourably if the available statistics are used carefully.

It is essential, therefore, that the tabulation of international comparisons of strike activity must be appraised with a full understanding of the definitional problems that render such comparisons meaningful and valid. This, in part, is the intention behind much of the interest shown in the compilation of disputes' statistics by the supra-national bodies such as the ILO, OECD and EEC. Each of these organisations has a commitment to an easier understanding of national differences and much of this can only be realised through better statistics.

The first real attempt at co-ordinating the statistics on industrial disputes came from the Third International Labour Office Conference of Labour Statisticians convened in 1926 under the auspices of the ILO. The conference laid down a set of guidelines by which member countries could collect their statistics on disputes.[7] The guidelines were not mandatory but merely advisory and countries were free to choose whether to use them or not. This freedom of choice meant that in some countries the guidelines were largely ignored. Others followed them on specific points but few took every phrase to heart. Yet despite the various degrees of uptake, it is clear that the guidelines have played an important part in shaping the collection of dispute statistics in many of the countries covered in this study. Without doubt, had they not been devised then international comparisons would be even more hazardous than they are at present.

The OECD much later on commissioned a thorough examination of the methods of measurement of industrial disputes in its member countries[8] and published the findings in Fisher, 1973.[9] The book looks at the problem of measurement from a broader view than just international comparability. Built into the study are the other associated economic factors which Fisher has used to partly explain the variations in stoppage activity. Strictly speaking, however, the book represents the best attempt hitherto at examining the measurement problems in the countries covered. The basic definitions given in the OECD book were updated by Creigh et al. in an article published in 1980.[10]

The most recent efforts at bringing together the methods of measurement in different countries have emanated from the EC and in particular the Statistical Office (SOEC), which commissioned comparative work on the eight member countries of Belgium, Denmark, France, the Federal Republic of Germany, Ireland, Italy, the Netherlands and the UK. The results have been published[11] with derived analyses for the four largest member countries (France, Germany (FRG), Italy and the UK), covering regional statistics[12] and measurement and trends over a long period.[13] Luxembourg was not given detailed coverage because that country did not have an established mechanism by whch it could record a strike or lockout. Thus there would appear to be no industrial disputes in Luxembourg, though the reliability of this conclusion is surely questionable in the absence of an information collection system?

The ILO guidelines

The ILO guidelines on what member countries should collect by way of statistics on industrial disputes was one of the first areas of statistical information to be tackled by that organisation and this led to a coherent package of results. Apart from statistics on wages and hours of work dealt with in part by the First International Conference of Labour Statisticians convened in 1923, most other important indicators such as employment, price indices and unemployment were tackled much later.[14] The guidelines on industrial disputes which emerged in 1926 have remained more or less intact until the present day.

As Sweet and Jackson point out, the ILO guidelines were primarily trying to establish a consistent approach to the collection of information, and information of both a quantitative and qualitative kind.[15] The quantifiable information would cover the main measures of strike activity such as the number of stoppages, workers involved, and working time lost, while the qualitative aspect would provide a broader, less precise insight into the nature of the stoppages through such classifications of the data as cause and method of settlement. Thus the ILO recommendations provide a comprehensive set of indicators which, if followed by member countries, would not only ensure a relatively complete perspective of stoppage activity, but would also ensure a high degree of comparability between countries.

The first task of the Conference was to establish a common definition of what was meant by an industrial dispute and the definition ultimately drawn up covered both strikes and lockouts explicitly (the definition has already been referred to on page 6). It was stated that where possible the statistics should be compiled separately for strikes and lockouts. The recommendations then went on to list the main measures of activity to be used as follows:

    number of disputes;
    number of establishments involved;
    number of workers involved;
    duration of the dispute;
    number of man-days lost.

There was no mention in the recommendations of counting those indirectly affected by the dispute (see Chapter 2) and it would, therefore, appear that the statisticians were limiting their coverage to direct effects only.

The guidelines went on to indicate what classifications of both number of establishments affected and man-days lost should be regularly compiled. The following were regarded as essential:

    the matter in dispute (i.e., the cause);
    the result of the dispute;
    the method of settlement;
    the industries affected;
    the importance of the disputes; and
    the amount of lost wages caused by the dispute.

On most of these classifications there was further information on what breakdowns to use and these will be discussed further under each appropriate heading in Chapter 2. Of all the listed classifications, the one which has been ignored by all nine countries covered in this study is the measure of the amount of wages lost by participants in the dispute. But then the whole area of the costs of disputes to both sides (employer and employee) has not been tackled by any of the countries.

It was also suggested in the recommendations that member countries should calculate both risk and frequency measures, the former using the measure of the number of full-time workers, and the latter using the number of disputes per 100,000 full-time workers; and that the relative severity of a dispute should be based on a measure of the number of man-days lost for every 10,000 full-time workers. This latter measure, as will be shown later, represents the most consistent measure of activity for use in the international comparison of dispute activity.

Finally, the recommendations concluded with advice on the frequency of collection and publication of this information. Broadly, it was suggested that the statistics be published at least once a year, but that the relevant information should be assembled and some of it published on a monthly basis, specifically information on the number of disputes.

In general there is a considerable amount of evidence that the guidelines have proved useful to member countries in formulating their statistical series, though it must be said that no one country of the nine covered here is actually producing a statistical series with measures and classifications identical to those recommended by the ILO. The collection of statistics on industrial disputes in individual countries tends to be more a result of the particular historical attitude towards the strike, with, for example, some countries still using a system of measurement that grew out of the view of strikes as a potential act of civil commotion (this being the case in Italy for example—see Chapter 9).

This point illustrates perhaps the most serious criticism of the ILO guidelines in that they made no attempt to cover the *method* of measurement of the disputes. There were no recommendations to countries on what agencies should ideally be used, whether employers should be asked for information or whether government officials should seek it out, or more basically should disputes of a certain size be excluded from the statistics? By omitting to cover such aspects of information provision, they gave member countries little guidance in developing their measurement systems and the result has been that even amongst a small group of nine developed countries such as those covered here, there are significant differences in the methods of measurement, which cause serious problems when the statistics so derived are compared internationally.

Of course it may be argued that the measurement of industrial disputes is done to satisfy national considerations and not for the benefit of international comparisons. It is true that in most countries there is a considerable amount of interest in using the national statistics to compare stoppage activity within regions, for example, and the available statistics can be successfully used for this purpose assuming that they are collected on a consistent basis and that a suitable comparative measure (such as working days lost per 1,000 workers) is used. However, such confined use of the statistics is rare. Most countries wish to compare their activity with that of their neighbours, as witnessed in the case of Germany (FRG), the UK and the USA for example, which all publish international comparisons of industrial disputes in their national statistical publications. When such comparisons are made, the problems of measurement are immediately elevated from the national level to the international level, requiring a fuller understanding of all aspects of the methods used.

Notes

1. See, for example, Knowles, K. G. J. C., *Strikes: A Study in Industrial Conflict* (Oxford, Basil Blackwell, 1952) or Handy, L. J., 'Absenteeism and attendance in the British coal-mining industry: an examination of post-war trends', *British Journal of Industrial Relations*, Vol. VI: 1 (1968).
2. Brown, W. (ed.), *The Changing Contours of British Industrial Relations* (Oxford, Basil Blackwell, 1981), see Chapter 5.
3. See Parker, S., *Workplace Industrial Relations 1972* (London, HMSO, 1974).
4. From the resolution concerning statistics of industrial disputes adopted by the Third International Conference of Labour Statisticians, 1926, reprinted as Chapter 9 in *International Recommendations on Labour Statistics* (Geneva, ILO, 1976).
5. Various press reports have covered the deliberations over the proposed plant and the major considerations. See, for example, *The Times*, 24 April 1981, p. 15, and 16 July 1981, p. 20. *The Economist*, 31 January 1981, p. 67 and 5 December 1981, pp. 79–80.
6. For a thorough discussion of the history of industrial relations in the UK car industry see Turner, H. A., Clack, G., and Roberts, G., *Labour Relations in the Motor Industry* (Cambridge, Cambridge University Press, 1967). More recently there has been a useful appraisal by previous car workers. Friedman, H. and Meredeen, S., *The Dynamics of Industrial Conflict: Lessons from Ford* (London, Croom Helm, 1980).

7. The conference covered, in addition to statistics on industrial disputes, those on family budget enquiries, classification of industries, and statistics of collective agreements.

8. The member countries covered are Australia, Austria, Belgium, Canada, Denmark, Finland, France, Federal Republic of Germany, Iceland, Ireland, Italy, Japan, the Netherlands, Norway, Spain, Sweden, the UK and the USA. (Note: The member countries excluded were Greece, Luxembourg, New Zealand, Portugal, Switzerland, Turkey and Yugoslavia).

9. Fisher, M., *The Measurement of Labour Disputes and their Economic Effects* (Paris, OECD, 1973).

10. Creigh, S., Donaldson, N. and Hawthorn, E. 'Stoppage activity in OECD countries', *Employment Gazette*, Vol. 88: 11 (November 1980).

11. Walsh, K., *Industrial Disputes: Methods and Measurement in the European Community* (Luxembourg, Eurostat, 1982).

12. Walsh, K., 'Industrial disputes activity in some EEC countries: a regional perspective', *Manpower Studies*, No. 3 (Autumn 1981).

13. Walsh, K., 'An analysis of strikes in four EEC countries', *Industrial Relations Journal*, Vol. 13: 4 (Winter 1982).

14. The Eighth International Conference of Labour Statisticians (1954) produced a series of recommendations on collecting employment and unemployment statistics, while price indices were covered in the earlier Sixth Conference held in 1947. The current recommendations for all these statistics are reproduced in the ILO publication of 1976, op. cit.

15. Sweet, T. G., and Jackson, D., *The Classification and Interpretation of Strike Statistics: An International Comparative Analysis* (University of Aston Management Centre, Working Paper No. 97, 1978).

2 DEFINITIONS AND MEASURES OF ACTIVITY

Like most other data series, to the uninitiated the statistics on stoppages of work can abound in jargon that at first sight may appear difficult to understand. The problem with stoppages data is compounded by two further factors. Firstly, they are an intrinsic part of the general field of industrial relations and as such contain many references, phrases and definitions applicable to that particular discipline, broadly defined. Secondly, the international comparison of stoppage statistics can bring into play the different interpretations imposed by each individual country. In most cases this does not present a problem, though in some circumstances even a slight alteration of emphasis can affect the meaning of the statistics, underlining the need for the user to be aware of the problems.

This chapter, therefore, isolates the main definitions that are used and explains what they mean. It also examines in more detail the main measures and classifications used in the statistics and explains any problems that the user of such statistics should be aware of. The substance of the chapter will provide the essential background information for understanding both the individual national chapters in Part II and the international comparison of methods of measurement discussed in the following chapter to this.

Types of action

The discussion of stoppage statistics is limited to strikes and lockouts only and does not include any of the other forms that industrial action can take. Nevertheless, it is still the case that there are various types of strikes and lockouts which are treated in different ways by each country in compiling the regular statistics on industrial disputes. The major variations are discussed below.

The general definition used to determine what constitutes a strike or a lockout has already been briefly discussed (p. 6). The strike, always initiated by the employees, is the most common form of action. Lockouts (that is, literally the shutting out of the workforce from their place of work) are thought to be much less common in practice, though in the absence of separate information in most countries on the incidence of such action, it is difficult to be precise about its extent. In fact the only country of the nine covered in this study that records and publishes the incidence of lockouts separately is Germany (FRG).

From the statistics in Germany, it would appear that the incidence is both high on occasion and at the same time significant in terms of working time lost. Taking the ten-year period 1972–81, there were 1,235 establishments recorded as being affected by a lockout (though these lockouts were concentrated into only five years as there were a further five years when none at all were recorded). In total, these accounted for approximately 24 per cent of all workers involved in both strikes and lockouts, but 44 per cent of total working days lost. In both 1978 and 1979 the number and scale of lockouts were such that they constituted even larger proportions of both workers involved and working days lost for each individual year than the averages for the whole ten-year period (see Chapter 7 for further details).

However, the case of Germany is almost certainly untypical of the other countries. Kennedy, for example, points out that German employers have been more disposed to using the lockout to counter employee claims than is the case in other countries, with lockouts occurring usually at the same time as a strike (that is, as a counter-measure).[1] In other countries lockouts are virtually unknown, and in France they are considered in most cases to be illegal. So it would be wrong to assume that other countries would experience lockout activity on a par with the German experience. But the problem always remains that in the absence of separate data it is difficult to say this with any degree of precision. Suffice it to say that all nine countries do attempt to include such action when it occurs and so the overall statistics should be as complete as possible.

Though the overall definition of a strike is relatively straight-forward, its very simplicity covers over the various types of strike that may be taken. Of course a simple definition is an asset in compiling the regular statistics, though in practice some types of strike cause serious problems of measurement.

Consider the case of the sit-in or occupation of the place of work, not an uncommon form of action in some countries as a desperate measure to protect jobs. Does such action constitute a strike or not? The fact is that the status of such action is not at all clear. It is certainly the case that workers have stopped work in response to a grievance, but the fact that they are still on the premises may preclude it from being counted as a strike. In any event, some countries have declared such action illegal on occasions, though in France, for example, the attitude of the courts has been distinctly ambivalent towards it.

There are no clear guidelines as how such disputes should be regarded when compiling the regular statistics in most countries and the decision to include them is generally taken by the statisticians compiling the series. In practice their incidence may be so small that they would have an imperceptible effect on the overall statistics anyway, but this is not always easy to see from the available data.

Direct/indirect effects

Those workers actively participating in a strike and usually instrumental in calling it would be those considered *directly* involved. The definition is normally only applied to workers at the establishment where the stoppage first began and is similarly applied in the case of lockouts, though clearly in such cases the workers affected would not be directly instrumental in starting the action.

In the case of many stoppages, however, the effects of the stoppage may not be confined simply to those directly involved. At the same establishment there will usually be *indirect* effects on other groups of workers who are forced out of their work because of the stoppage by other workers. Typically the workers directly involved in such situations will be key personnel in such functions as maintenance staff, perhaps looking after production tracks. All is fine for those working on the track until it breaks down, then, in the absence of the maintenance staff to repair it, the workers on the track are laid off.

Most of the nine countries covered in this study measure and include any indirect effects, the exceptions being France, Germany (FRG) and Italy where such effects are excluded. In the remaining six countries, however, only the UK separates out such indirect effects and hence provides the only indication of its scale, which may provide a useful indication of the extent of it in other countries.

Taking the UK data over the ten-year period 1972–81, the number of workers indirectly involved in all recorded strikes and lockouts amounted to approximately 19.5 per cent of the total number of workers involved, both directly and indirectly. There was some variation in the proportion of all workers involved, accounted for by indirect effects from year to year, but generally each year involved a significant amount of such involvement (for more details see Chapter 11).

The implications for the statistics produced by those three countries which do not measure indirect effects are clear. It is reasonable to assume that industries in other countries such as France,

Germany (FRG) and Italy, which have fairly similar industrial structures to that of the UK, would experience similar levels of indirect effects. It would seem, therefore, that in the measure of workers involved these three countries would be deficient to the order of one-fifth. The effect on man-days lost is less clear and the UK statistics do not isolate the man-days lost attributable to indirect effects. Given the fact that in most cases the indirect effects would tend to operate with a variable time lag after the first direct action (as machines break down and are not repaired, for example, or stocks of components become exhausted), then it would seem that man-days lost would be appreciably less than this estimate of one-fifth, but nevertheless a significant amount in most cases.

Secondary effects

When the effects of a stoppage at one establishment indirectly affect the continuation of work at another establishment, this becomes a *secondary* effect. In many cases it will be caused by such factors as a shortage of components from a major supplier which brings production to a halt, or perhaps a transport strike which prevents goods from leaving the plant, the resultant stock-piling stopping further production. Whatever the cause, the important point is that the establishment which is suffering the secondary effect does so involuntarily.

Clearly there are many common characteristics between secondary effects and indirect effects, not the least being the difficulty in measuring both. In fact the problems of accurate measurement are considered so immense with secondary effects that none of the nine countries attempt it. Thus there are no statistics on secondary effects at all, even though it is reasonable to assume that in many instances these will be significant in terms of both workers affected and man-days lost as a result, especially given the concentration of stoppages in those industries vulnerable to external effects (more fully discussed in Chapter 15).

Official/unofficial action

The distinction between what is called *official* industrial action and unofficial action tends to vary in each country and is frequently a function of the relative trade union structure that exists. Official action, taken at its most simplistic level, is that action which has the full recognition of the executive committee of the appropriate trade union. Along with recognition goes support, and this can take the form not only of moral support but also financial assistance from central union funds for those involved with the action. Therefore, given the importance of such financial support to the strength and solidarity of a strike, the measure of official recognition becomes an important component indicator of strike propensity.

By definition, those stoppages which are not given official recognition are classified as unofficial, though such a simple dichotomy can be misleading. Many non-official disputes in the sense outlined above, nevertheless do have the support of the local branch of the relevant trade union and in some cases this support may extend to the regional level. Again, though, this is a generalisation and there is considerable variation to be found in the interpretation of official or unofficial action even in the small number of countries examined in this study.

Perhaps the extreme case is that of Germany where the existing labour law (discussed more fully in Chapter 16) imposes strict conditions on the right to call a strike. One of the prime conditions for a strike to be regarded as legal is that it must have the authorisation of the national union, in other words it must be official. However, the strictness of the conditions even extends into the individual trade union rules regarding strike action. For example, the DGB (Deutscher Gewerkschaftsbund) the Federal Republic's trade union confederation,[2] has a rule that before a strike can be put into effect, not only must it be approved by the national union to comply with labour law, but in addition at least 75 per cent of employees must vote in favour of such action through a secret ballot.[3]

Given the differences in interpretation of what constitutes official or unofficial action, it is not surprising to note that only one country of the nine, the UK, actually attempts to identify both types of action separately in its official statistics. Two other countries, Ireland and the Netherlands, do include a category in the classification by cause of dispute which isolates trade union involvement, though this does not differentiate between local and national involvement and hence, given the definition of official action that tends to be used, cannot be taken as an indicator of official and unofficial action that is comparative to the UK data.

The USA shows stoppages by the level of affiliation with the major labour organisations (see Chapter 12), but does not show whether the action is officially recognised or not.

Using the figures from the UK over the period 1971–80, it is possible to get some idea of the extent of official compared to unofficial action. The averages for the ten-year period are shown in Table 2.1. Clearly, though the percentage of recorded stoppages with

Table 2.1 Official and unofficial action compared
(UK, average percentages over period 1971–80)

	Official	Unofficial
Stoppages	4.7	95.3
Workers involved	42.4	57.6
Working days lost	61.0	29.0

Source: *Employment Gazette,* Department of Employment.

official recognition is small at 4.7 per cent, they account for disproportionate numbers of workers involved (42.4 per cent) and working days lost (61 per cent). This is perhaps not surprising given the fact that official stoppages will tend to be backed with financial support (from union funds) for those involved and hence will tend to be of longer duration, both factors contributing to the relatively large amount of time lost. Further details of this series of data can be found in Table 11.1. Though the UK is the only country of the nine to separate official action from unofficial, all nine actually measure both types of action.

Sympathetic action

Potentially many instances of strike action can be due to other groups of workers giving support to a group already on strike. The cause, therefore, is one of solidarity with fellow workers and the objective may be to either simply show this support, or through a combined effort bring further pressure to bear on the employer. Many of these strikes involve a number of different establishments belonging to one corporation. For example, if workers at one plant within the company are taking action then additional support might be given by one or more plants in the group to put more weight behind the demands. Such an approach has been popular in, for example, the motor car industry, where stoppages can spread very quickly.[4]

Though all nine countries include any sympathetic action in their stoppage statistics, only those six countries classifying by cause of stoppage would be able to identify it separately. However, in the statistics for the USA, those stoppages taken in sympathy with other strikers would be classified under the cause of the original dispute and hence are not identified separately as sympathetic stoppages.

Using the available data from some of the other countries, however, enables the extent of any sympathetic action to be gauged. Table 2.2 sets out the relevant figures for four countries, Belgium, Ireland, Italy and the UK. They show that apart from the case of

Italy, where 4.1 per cent of all working days lost were due to sympathetic action, the three other countries show very small proportions with 1.3 per cent in Belgium, 0.3 per cent in the UK and only 0.1 per cent in Ireland. However, in interpreting these figures the problem remains that of adequately identifying sympathetic action, especially at the establishment level, since a lot of seemingly supportive action can be nothing more than other groups of workers joining in a dispute which they sympathize with and hope to materially benefit from in due course.

Table 2.2 Proportion of sympathetic action
(percentage of total working days lost)

	Sympathetic action
Belgium (1972–8)	1.3
Ireland (1972–81)	0.1
Italy (1972–80)	4.1
UK (1973–81)	0.3

Source: National statistics.

Political strikes

The term 'political strike' is usually taken to mean that the cause of the stoppage is not directly to do with the strikers' place or conditions of work, but has a wider relevance. The term 'political' can be misleading in this context and perhaps 'protest' is better, since in most cases the stoppages falling into this definition will be a protest response by workers.

The nine countries show differing treatments of political protest stoppages. Four of the nine (Belgium, France, the UK and the USA) specifically exclude such action from the statistics, limiting them to issues connected purely with the terms and conditions of work. Of the other five, though any protest action is measured, the treatment of political strikes is variable. For example, in Germany such strikes are considered illegal anyway, while the opposite situation exists in Italy where the use of the short protest stoppage is very common and an established practice.

In the case of Italy, the classification by cause of dispute (see Table 9.4) does not specifically identify political or protest stoppages. However, there is a category of 'stoppages by other causes' which is considered to be mainly for those stoppages of a political nature,[5] and over the period 1975–80 approximately 21 per cent of all working days lost fell into this classification. Clearly Italy is an exceptional case in its experience of the political strike, but in other countries where such action is permissible (in particular Belgium, France and the UK, which all experience political protest stoppages regularly) their exclusion could cause serious problems of under-estimation.

There are strong grounds for including such action when it occurs, despite the insistence in some countries that stoppage statistics should be confined to those disputes concerned with the terms and conditions of work. Though most protest action on a large scale (for example, national strikes) may ostensibly seem politically motivated, in most cases there will be underlying causes fundamentally concerned with terms and conditions of work. A national protest stoppage over, say, a wage freeze is primarily concerned with the pay of individual strikers and its appearance as a political stoppage will arise out of the direction of the protest towards the instigators of the measure, namely the government.

Measures of activity

Basically there are four main measures of activity commonly used in statistics on industrial disputes, though not all four are regularly used in all of the nine countries covered in this study. They are as follows:

> number of stoppages;
> number of establishments affected;
> number of workers involved; and
> working time lost.

The four measures are included in the ILO guidelines and form the basis for classifications of the data by, for example, cause or industry groups affected. As such, they are the most important ingredients of the data collection exercise, being the end product which ultimately permits the dimensions of strike activity to be examined.

Apart from the fact that not all countries produce statistics for each of the four measures, there are further problems to be encountered in comparing the data in those countries that do since each is often subjected to different interpretation. Below, each of the four main measures are explained in detail, conceptually at first and then with some discussion of comparability. Further coverage is given to the measures in each country in Part II, while Chapter 3 discusses the full implications for international comparisons looking at measures and classifications collectively.

Number of stoppages

The number of stoppages should measure the quantity of separately identifiable stoppages of work over a given period of time, taking care to avoid any double-counting of stoppages affecting several establishments but with a common cause or starting point. The ILO guidelines help a little to understand what should be measured by stating that any stoppages '. . . organised or directed by one person or organisation' should be counted as a single stoppage.[6] This, in fact, is really the only way that stoppages can and should be measured, though it tells little of the type of stoppages that are experienced.

Fisher calls this a 'hybrid' solution to the measurement problem in that it attempts to solve the dilemma of how to measure the number of stoppages by the apparently simple solution of counting all those with a common cause as one.[7] It probably is a hybrid, but nevertheless one which avoids much of the ambiguity that would be involved in determining stoppages on any other basis. Ideally it should be used alongside some measure of the number of establishments involved to illustrate the difference in the two measures, though in practice only four of the nine countries actually do this (Belgium, France, Germany and Ireland).

France, however, has an altogether wider concept which is applied to the statistics. Here those stoppages which clearly have a wider cause or effect and which by their very nature are difficult to pin down to a specific industry, firm, or location, are counted separately as generalised disputes (*conflits généralisés*). These disputes would be counted as one stoppage, but would, by their separation, be instantly identified as having broader impact. Chapter 6 discusses the concept more fully.

Of course the measurement of the number of stoppages can never be straightforward whatever the measurement rules are. Many stoppages will be of very short duration, perhaps lasting for only one or two hours or perhaps a series of one hour stoppages over a period of a few days. These in particular can cause serious problems for those providing the necessary information on the stoppage (usually the employer) as well as for the statisticians faced with the task of compiling the regular statistics. One way to avoid some of this confusion, therefore, is the adoption of a minimum size under which stoppages would *not* be included in the statistics. The minimum adopted would be at a point which would ensure that only the smaller disputes would be excluded, those which only contribute marginally to the overall measure of time lost. Of course in defining size, it is important to remember that it is a combination of duration and the number of workers involved (both directly and indirectly), so ideally any minimum should be defined in terms of a combination of these aspects.

Six of the nine countries in this study impose a minimum size for inclusion, though not all are the same size. The other three include all stoppages which come to the attention of the relevant collection agency. This inevitably leads to problems when comparing the number of stoppages internationally, though in reality even where all stoppages are theoretically included, the majority of the smaller ones will go unrecorded anyway simply through escaping the mechanisms of recording.

Establishments affected

The number of individual establishments involved in a stoppage should be more straightforward to measure than the number of stoppages. Even though a stoppage affecting a number of different establishments may have a common cause or starting point, each establishment affected by a stoppage of work will be counted. The ILO guidelines were more explicit on the point and defined the basis of the count as the 'technical unit' as defined in the national census of industries. In other words, the measure should take full account of those establishments in different locations but also those alongside each other but which nevertheless operate autonomously.

In practice, however, things are never quite as simple as they appear and there are many common problems in both measuring the number of stoppages and establishments affected. For example, what happens in the case of a so-called 'rotating strike' (sometimes called a revolving strike) when the employees at different locations take it in turns to strike, perhaps with long intervals in between? The same dispute is common to all the series of stoppages, but the individual stoppages are spaced over a long period of time and may appear wrongly as separate disputes. Similarly the individual establishment affected may be counted separately even though they are not strictly technical entities (for example, individual hospitals within a national health service). Basically, there are no clear guidelines on what to do in such a situation, certainly there are none at an international level. Interpretation of individual cases will be dependent on the established practice in each country and it is unlikely, therefore, that there will be a common denominator.

Exploring further the relationship between the number of stoppages and establishments involved, it is possible using the statistics from the three countries which measure both to get some idea of the ratio between the two. Table 2.3 shows the number of stoppages, establishments affected and the average number of establishments per stoppage over a ten-year period for France and Ireland, and over nine years for Belgium. The average number of establishments affected is the highest in France at 7.1 and this covers all types of stoppage including *conflits généralisés*. For the smaller countries the corresponding figures are much lower, with 2.6 establishments per stoppage in Belgium and 1.3 establishments in Ireland, no doubt reflecting some of the size difference between the three countries. This is only a crude measure of the relationship between these two indicators of activity, but it does serve to show the inherent differences in both.

Table 2.3 Stoppages and establishments affected compared

	Number of stoppages	Establishments affected	Average establishments per stoppage
Belgium (1972–80)	1,877	4,832	2.6
France (1972–81)	34,470	246,307	7.1
Ireland (1972–81)	1,531	2,050	1.3

Source: National statistics.

Workers involved

The number of participants in a stoppage of work constitute the workers directly involved as well as those passively or indirectly affected: put out of work by a stoppage involving another group or groups of workers. It has already been stated that not all countries measure both those directly and indirectly involved, which of itself causes problems in international comparisons. Whatever measure of worker involvement is used, however, it cannot quantify the true degree of active support for a stoppage. In almost all cases where workers are brought out on strike, there will be a number of the participants who do not wholly support the action but nevertheless come out in fear of intimidation or other recriminatory action. In addition to this problem, however, any international comparisons are affected further by the different ways of measuring workers involved used in some of the countries.

The ILO guidelines recommended that the number of workers involved should be calculated by taking an average of the number of 'vacancies' caused each day (or where this was impractical, each week) by the stoppage for its total duration. The concept of vacancies meant that numbers would be calculated on the basis of the normal workforce less those who reported for work and were working normally, the residual being the vacancies which would normally be filled by the striking workers. The recommendation made no explicit statement concerning the direct or indirect effects of the stoppage and the implication appears to be that all effects should be included.

As far as it is possible to accurately ascertain, it appears that seven of the nine countries covered use a method of calculation similar to the ILO averaging method. Of the two remaining countries, the UK and the USA, there are two clearly different methods of calculation used and it will be demonstrated that application of the three methods to a simple example produce three different results.

In the UK, the normal way of calculating the number of workers involved takes the maximum number of workers that took part during the course of the stoppage, even if some participants only took a limited part in the action, say striking for two days out of a strike which lasted for five days in total. The US method differs slightly in that it takes the highest number of workers affected on any one day of the stoppage.

The different results yielded by the three different methods are best illustrated by use of the diagram in Figure 2.1. Here the details of a stoppage have been simplified showing that at the point of

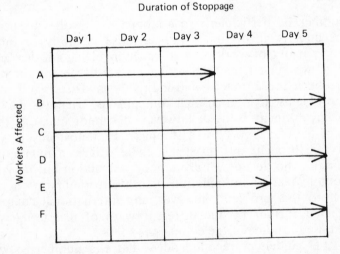

Figure 2.1 Measuring number of workers affected

measurement it had lasted for a maximum of five working days (horizontal axis) and involved (with differing inputs of time) six individuals (A–F). The solid horizontal arrows represent the involvement in working days of each individual. For example, individual A joined the stoppage at the beginning but went back to work after three days, whereas individual D was not affected until day three, but stayed out until the end of day five.

Taking the ILO averaging method first, its application to the example in Figure 2.1 would establish the number of workers involved as the total workers involved each day (i.e. twenty), divided by the number of days the stoppage lasted for (i.e. five days). The number of workers involved would, therefore, be *four*. The UK method would render a different result of *six* workers involved because that is the maximum number of individuals who have been affected in some way during the course of the stoppage, regardless of the varying degrees of involvement. Finally, the US method would fall in between the two, with a figure of *five* workers involved, by taking the day of the stoppage when most workers were affected (i.e. day three or day four).

Different results from application of the three different methods will arise in most cases where the stoppage lasts longer than a day and during its course participation in it (of either a direct or indirect nature) varies. The latter condition is probably more common than may at first appear. The support for a strike will tend to be strong at the beginning, but will usually weaken as it drags on, with financial pressures, for example, forcing some participants back to work (assuming the absence of other persuasive factors such as picketing which may prevent this from happening). Similarly, any workers laid off through the indirect effects of the stoppage will tend to be affected well into the dispute when, for example, machines start to break down or supplies of parts become exhausted.

The longer a stoppage continues, of course, the more difficult it becomes for either the employer or the agency responsible for collecting the statistics to keep an accurate track of numbers of workers involved. What can be said, however, is that in the case of the UK and to a lesser extent the USA, their methods of calculating worker involvement will produce consistently higher estimates than if the ILO averaging recommendation had been adopted. However, short of going back to raw data and recalculating the figures, it is impossible to estimate with any accuracy the likely size of the discrepancy.

One final point about measuring the number of workers involved needs to be made. This concerns the treatment of part-time workers who may be either directly or indirectly affected by a stoppage of work. All countries seem to count the number of 'heads' involved rather than attempting to make any assessment of their whole-time equivalents, of itself a difficult exercise given the variability in the number of hours normally worked by part-timers. This may be a satisfactory method when simply looking at workers involved (though a distinction between full- and part-time participants would be useful), but it will inevitably cause major problems if these figures are then used as a multiplicative factor with the duration of the stoppage to calculate the total amount of lost time. It would always produce exaggerated estimates of working days lost.

Working time lost

The measurement of the amount of working time lost as a result of a stoppage is frequently intended to provide some measure of its economic costs. The usual method is to use the total number of working man-days lost due to the stoppage. In the nine countries covered here only Italy deviates from this normal practice, preferring to use working hours lost instead. Though hours may provide a more precise measure of time lost, this method does cause a few problems when it comes to making comparisons with other countries using man-days. The simple device of dividing by eight (based on an average eight-hour working day) cannot take into account the variations in normal hours worked across various occupations or industries, for example.

The ILO guidelines suggested that man-days lost should be the measure used and that this should be based on a daily count of the number of 'vacancies' caused by the stoppage, each vacancy representing the man-day of work lost. The conference recommendations went on to say that where a daily count was not possible, then the average number of workers involved during the course of the dispute should be used instead. Using the example in Figure 2.1, application of either of these two methods of calculation would produce the same result of twenty working days lost.

In those cases where the number of workers involved is calculated in a different way to the averaging process, as in the UK and the USA where the maximum number and the peak number are used respectively, then the calculation of days lost will clearly reveal different results. There will also be significant differences caused by the inclusion or exclusion of indirect effects at the same establishment where the stoppage is taking place, such that those countries which exclude indirect action (and there are three of them) will underestimate the total working time lost.

Also, the usual method of measurement used for assessing time lost due to a stoppage cannot take into account the incidence of any overtime normally worked, or adjust for those members of the affected workforce with a normal working day below the standard eight hours or its equivalent. Where levels of overtime worked are comparatively high (such as in the UK where the average number of overtime hours worked per week by manual workers is put at about five hours),[8] then in most cases the estimates of total working time lost will be underestimates of the actual losses of work caused by the stoppage. The opposite problem applies to part-time workers, where their shorter working day will lead to overestimates of time lost in cases where such workers are affected by a stoppage.

Finally, there remains the question of how to treat any periods of normal non-working which fall during the course of a stoppage? In the main these will be public holidays, weekends or annual shutdowns which, under normal circumstances, are not worked anyway and so should not be counted in any assessment of days lost through the dispute. This fact is generally accepted by the nine countries covered in this study and so, in theory, no problems should arise. However, there is the ever present problem of misunderstanding and miscalculation which can be especially the case when the compilers of the statistics have to rely on information received or, worse still, as is sometimes the case in a number of the countries, if the facts are gleaned from press reports, for example.

Minimum size for inclusion

The considerable measurement problems that may be encountered with measuring working time lost for a small dispute is overcome to some extent by the application of a minimum size for inclusion. Those stoppages falling below the threshold will be excluded from the statistics and, in most cases, will not be recorded at all. Six countries of the nine covered here have such a minimum size, which in most cases is based on duration (in working days) of the stoppage, and workers involved, or a combination of the two to give a measure of working time lost. Chapter 3 discusses the differences in national criteria in more detail. However, it is interesting to point out that from January 1982, the USA imposed an even more restrictive exclusion level for recording purposes, such that only those stoppages involving 1,000 or more workers will be measured (see Chapter 12).

The changes introduced in the USA underline the other considerations in national governments which favour the use of a minimum size criterion. The vast majority of stoppages are of very short duration and so to include them all would involve a considerable amount of effort by both the employer (in most cases the provider of the information) and the agency with responsibility for collating the data. Yet overall, their contribution to the proxy measure of the cost of the dispute, the amount of working time lost, is relatively small. For example, in the case of the USA shown in Table 2.4 (taken before the introduction of the new threshold for inclusion) over the period 1976–80 on average less than 0.2 per cent of all stoppages accounted for over one-third of all man-days lost, with small variations from year to year.

Table 2.4 Contribution of largest stoppages to working time lost (USA, stoppages involving 10,000 or more workers)

	Number of stoppages	Percentage of all stoppages	Number of man-days lost (000s)	Percentage of all man-days lost
1976	23	0.2	14,043	37.1
1977	18	0.2	9,886	27.6
1978	11	0.1	13,537	36.7
1979	11	0.1	9,268	26.7
1980	14	0.2	12,256	36.8

Source: Analysis of Work Stoppages, US Bureau of Labor Statistics.

The argument goes, therefore, that by having such a threshold to determine inclusion in the statistics, most working time lost is captured but at the saving of considerable resources on data collection and analysis. Therefore, given the variable application of such minimum criteria across countries and the variation of individual criteria used between those countries that do so, it is generally accepted that the best comparative measure to use is the number of working days lost. The detailed examination of international trends presented in Part III is therefore largely dependent on this measure as the basis for its comparisons.

Data classifications

The importance of the classifications of stoppage data is self-evident. They add depth and understanding to the individual disputes and go a long way to explain the cause and nature of the activity over a long period of analysis. Inevitably any classification will involve some degree of rationalisation such that, for example, cause of dispute will be a series of broad categories into which some stoppages might only just fit.

As already pointed out in the previous chapter, the ILO guidelines were quite explicit on the type and nature of the classifications that should be applied to at least two of the main measures of activity, the number of establishments affected and the number of working days lost. To recap, they suggested that the list should include classifications by cause, industries affected, size of dispute, the result and method of settlement as well as some calculation of the amount of wages lost by those involved. In addition, it was recommended that the duration of all disputes should be calculated and be based on the number of working days lost. The guidelines went into detail about the categories to use under each individual heading, and these will be discussed as appropriate below.

The guidelines further went on to suggest that there should be some additional consistent measures that could be more successfully used especially in international comparisons of the data. These should concentrate on assessing what was called the 'exposure to risk', in other words that the frequency and severity rates should be calculated. Both indicators are simply expressions of man-days lost and number of disputes in terms of the size of the employed labour force and, in fact, application of such a divisor is really the only way to get meaningful data for international comparisons.

In reality, the range of classifications to be found amongst the nine countries is more extensive than the range recommended by the ILO, though none of the countries uses the 'amount of wages' lost category. In addition to those listed, some countries produce the following classifications:

occupations affected;
regions (for smaller local areas).

There are also variations to be found in the types of classification used under the broader headings of the 'importance of disputes' (for example, some list individually the principal disputes) and 'methods of settlement', and such variations are discussed below. Not all countries produce all the classifications of their national data and some produce only one or two. The coverage is fully discussed in Chapter 3.

Cause

The ILO recommended that member countries should classify some of the main measures of activity according to the matter in dispute or, in other words, the cause of the stoppage. It went on to list suggested sub-groupings within two broad sub-headings of (a) disputes related to collective bargaining, and (b) disputes not related to collective bargaining. Under the first of these categories would fall two further groupings: those disputes concerning trade unionism or refusal to conclude a collective agreement; and those concerning conditions of employment, itself sub-divided into four specific issues of: wages, hours of work, engagement or dismissal and a catchment category of 'other issues'. For the (b) category above, those disputes not related to collective bargaining, there were three suggested sub-groups of: sympathetic disputes; political disputes; and others.

For the six countries of the nine that actually attempt an assessment by cause, there is no evidence of any strict adherence to the ILO guidelines. In fact within the six there is considerable variation in the number of categories used. However, for all the countries, whatever categories of cause are used in the official statistics, there will always be the difficult task of attempting to condense a large number of different causes into a much smaller number of broader categories.

Any stoppage of work is the result of the coming together of a complex series of events amongst which it may be difficult to discern one key issue as being the catalyst to the action. This of itself brings into question the value of any classification by cause. However, Batstone *et al.* go further than this and attribute the limited value of the official statistics on the cause of stoppages to the fact that the data collectors depend on the reason given to them by others.[9] In other words, the statistics depend on the accuracy of the statements emerging from employers in the main, with the initiators and chief participants in the action, the workers, having little if any input into the official statistics.

That there are differences in the interpretation of particular strike situations by management on the one hand and workers on the other, seems to be without doubt. Clearly in a case where, for example, a strike has started over what might be categorised as an issue over pay, simple acceptance of this fact would tend to mask the sequence of events leading up to the call for industrial action. There may have been intransigence over the issue on the part of management, or more simply there may have been antipathy between the union leader and his negotiating opposite number. In such a situation pay might appear as the ostensible cause, but the true underlying cause could be very different and certainly less allied to a concern with terms and conditions of employment than would appear.

Moreover, reliance on a management categorisation by cause will tend to conceal any situation where that management has been instrumental in causing the dispute, but then again a worker or union response would probably render similarly biased results. The ideal, perhaps, is to have a dual series of statements published from both the employer and the worker or union side, so that any differences could be instantly identified. Of the nine countries, only the USA has attempted to collect these two views simultaneously by sending out a questionnaire requesting details of the stoppage to both the management and the union (or unions) of the establishment on strike. The problem is that in the vast majority of cases it is only the management questionnaire which is returned and thus the US Bureau of Labor Statistics is forced to base its data on mainly management information.

Thus the classification by cause can at best be only an indicator of the types of issue that might lie behind the stoppages recorded. In using them, therefore, it must be remembered that in most cases the strike is the ultimate weapon which is only invoked after a long series of preliminary effort has gone into finding a solution to the dispute. The cause of any strike, therefore, must lie in this complex series of events that precede the measurable action, and in most cases these will not be revealed by any classification by cause.

Industries affected

In order to establish those sectors of industry which are most prone to stoppage activity, the ILO conference recommended that countries should classify their statistics by the main industrial groupings. However, there was little if any emphasis on the co-ordination of the industry groups to be used by each country, this being left up to the 'domain of national statistics', as it was called. Unfortunately, the conference overlooked, or perhaps chose to ignore, the sometimes significant differences to be found in national industrial classifications which make international comparisons more difficult than they really need to be.

The tendency amongst countries to use their own national industrial classification is, perhaps, understandable given that

most other types of economic information such as unemployment, earnings or production statistics will be classified on a
similar basis. Therefore, to ensure the comparability of the
statistical series within the country must be the primary objective. As a result, little use is made of the two existing international classifications, the ISIC (International Standard Industrial
Classification) or, for EEC countries, the NACE (General Industrial Classification of Economic Activities within the European
Communities), except by the international bodies themselves in
their attempt to standardise groupings for their own statistical
series.

Most countries produce only a limited range of industrial
groupings for their strike statistics, since most activity is concentrated in only a few of the more strike-prone industry groups
(see Chapter 15). The problem is, however, that in those countries
where there is use of a minimum size for inclusion in the official
statistics, this will tend to automatically exclude those sectors of
industry where the size structure of firms is small in comparison
to other sectors. For example, the distributive sector has a high
proportion of small retail outlets which may suffer small strikes
which escape the recording threshold. On the other hand, the
vehicles sector will be composed of a small number of large
manufacturing units which, in the event of a stoppage, would
tend to suffer large numbers of workers involved and, consequently, man-days lost.

The problem of the compatibility of national industrial classifications is evident from the appropriate statistical tables annexed
to each national chapter in Part II. Each uses the normal breakdown into the groups that usually appear in the published
statistical sources in each country.

Apart from this problem of compatibility of classifications, the
main factor which is a potential source of anguish for the user
of the statistics remains that of those stoppages which affect more
than one industry simultaneously. In such cases, the normal
practice is to apportion the main measures of activity accordingly,
but inevitably there will be problems in ensuring a completely
accurate apportionment, with the problem becoming more acute
the more industry groups involved. Thus France does not publish
details of those stoppages which cut across a number of sectors
(known as *conflits généralisés*), limiting any industrial analyses to
those with a clearly identifiable group and location (discussed
further in Chapter 6). This is exceptional practice, however, and
most countries attempt some apportionment where necessary.

Occupations affected

There are considerable difficulties to be encountered in attempting to assess the occupational groups involved in the stoppages, largely due to the multiplicity of occupations and the problem of definition in most industries. Because of this the ILO guidelines, for example, make no mention of such a classification and amongst the nine countries covered here there is no comprehensive classification available.

To some extent the range of occupations affected by a stoppage can be gauged by the industries affected. In other words, if, for example, there is a strike in the coal-mining sector then it is reasonable to assume that the occupations affected will include primarily miners, as well as some other groups of workers perhaps less specific to that industry. However, such an assessment will not show the groups initiating the strike, or differentiate between those directly and indirectly involved, so the details will be of limited value.

In at least three of the nine countries, however, it is possible to get some idea of the main occupational groups involved. In Ireland, the UK and the USA, details are published of the major disputes (usually in terms of size) over a period, listing the main occupational groups of workers affected. The Irish statistics in fact list all the disputes recorded and the groups affected on a quarterly stencilled sheet with limited circulation, though such information is not consolidated into a classified grouping for the main publication. Also, given the different groupings used by each country, it would be very difficult to compare occupations affected, even amongst the three with some information to compare.

Regions

There is a considerable amount of interest in the spatial distribution of stoppage activity in all countries. A large part of this stems from the interest shown by employers, as Walsh points out,[10] especially those multinational employers concerned with the location of new capital investments. To some extent depending on the industry concerned, the general industrial relations ethos of a particular area will be an important input to the eventual choice of location.

In most cases, however, the published statistics only relate to the usual standard planning regions in each country, for example the nine Belgian provinces or the eleven *Landern* in Germany. In the USA, the fifty states plus the District of Columbia are used as the basic spatial breakdown, aggregated into ten broader regions (see

Chapter 12). Only France provides a more detailed breakdown beyond her twenty-two standard regions in the ninety-six *départements*, but for only those stoppages clearly identifiable as locally based (*conflits localisés*). In all other countries, there is an attempt to apportion both number of workers affected and working days lost to the appropriate regions for those stoppages which affect a number of regions simultaneously. The basis for this apportionment is the location of the affected establishment.

Duration of stoppage

The length of time for which a stoppage lasts, or its duration, is an important classification for all countries. In fact, the ILO regarded this as one of its main measures of activity, though in reality it must be seen as a basic, though important classification of the data. The relative importance of this classification mainly rests on its use as a multiplicative factor which, together with the number of workers involved, determines the total number of working days (or hours) lost.

The ILO guidelines suggested that it be measured in terms of the number of working days and should cover the whole length of the stoppage on an establishment basis. This is in fact what all nine countries except Italy do. In Italy there is a more precise measure of duration, using the number of hours of work lost. However, though more precise, the need to convert hours into days lost for comparisons with other countries does involve some broad assumptions about the average length of the Italian working day. In all cases the day or hour of measurement is the normal working period and does not include any assessment of extra working such as overtime, no matter how established such working practice might be.

For those countries that publish analyses of the main measures of activity by duration (in fact, seven of the nine do so), comparability of the data is not a problem, given the particular circumstances of Italy outlined above. All tend to use bands of days lost which lend themselves to straightforward comparison. The main problems will stem from the application of a minimum size criteria based on duration, such as exists in part of those criteria used in Germany, Ireland, the UK and the USA. This will automatically exclude the shorter stoppages (usually those lasting less than one working day) from the statistics in those countries. However, of the four main measures, the number of stoppages will be affected much more than the remaining three and so for the latter measure it is less of a problem.

Importance of dispute

The relative importance of a stoppage is, in effect, a synonym for the relative size of the stoppage and is measured in a number of different ways. The ILO guidelines recommend that all disputes should be classified according to four criteria: the number of establishments affected; the number of workers involved; the duration of the stoppage; and the number of man-days lost as a result. Further, more explicit details are given of the categories that should be used under each of these headings, all involving bands of, for example, workers involved or man-days lost.

A further measure of the importance of a dispute is published by two of the nine countries covered here, in the UK and the USA. In these two countries, tables are compiled on the principal disputes occurring during the year being covered. The criteria for inclusion in the UK is if the stoppage exceeds a total of 5,000 working days lost while in the USA the threshold is 10,000 or more workers involved. In both cases the disputes are covered in great detail, listing such aspects as specific locations of the establishments affected, the trade union involved (if any) and more descriptive details of such things as cause and settlement arrangements. It has already been demonstrated (see page 30) that these few major stoppages can account for a large proportion of the total working time lost due to all stoppages and so they assume a prominent role in the explanation of strike activity over the period covered.

Outcomes

Details of the end result of a dispute are particularly useful in understanding the efficacy of such action. The ILO, recognising this need, suggested that disputes should be classified according to the method of settlement. It listed three major categories as follows:

(a) disputes settled by direct negotiations between the two parties;
(b) disputes settled by the medium of a third party; and
(c) disputes terminated without successful negotiations.

Under (b) were also listed four different sub-categories covering the various types of arbitration or conciliation used.

However, despite the existence of the guidelines, only two countries, the Netherlands and the USA, bother to compile exact details of methods of settlement. In the case of the Netherlands the analysis is broad, consisting of three categories similar to those recommended by the ILO. In the case of the USA, there was, prior to the introduction of the revised measurement criteria (see Chapter 12), a much more detailed analysis.

In the USA, there are six types of settlement categories with the addition of a residual category for those disputes with insufficient information to determine the method of settlement. The classification is supplemented by detailed analyses of the various types of mediation used (for example, government or private mediation) in those disputes resolved in this way. Another analysis covers the procedures that were to be enacted in those disputes which had not been settled even though the stoppage had ended. The US statistics are, therefore, quite unique amongst the nine countries in their depth of coverage on the outcome of the disputes, but in the absence of similar statistics in other countries, they cannot be compared internationally.

Other classifications

In addition to the main classifications of the data listed and described above, there are a small number of additional ones that can be added to the list, but they mainly emanate only from the USA. For example, these may involve the analysis of the contractual status of the participants in the dispute (whether they are at the stage of re-negotiating an agreement, for example), or the involvement of trade unions in the dispute. Where appropriate, these additional classifications are discussed under the national chapters in Part II, though they are also set out in the context of comparability in Chapter 3.

Finally, the main classifications are frequently cross-classified in the published statistics (such as cause of dispute by industry group, for example) and these can add considerably to the understanding of the dimensions of stoppage activity. Unfortunately the cross-classifications used by each country, both in their extent and nature, tend to vary considerably which does significantly inhibit their value in international comparisons. Nevertheless, it would be possible to compare in some cases, using just a selected few of the nine countries covered. But the true value of these cross-classifications lies more in their contribution to understanding national trends and in this they are an invaluable asset to the more common dual classifications.

Notes

1. Kennedy, T., *European Labor Relations* (Lexington, D. C. Heath, 1980), p. 181.

2. The DGB had an estimated affiliated membership in 1980 of approximately 7.9 million representing about 84 per cent of total union membership in that year. More details can be found in Chapter 16.
3. See Kennedy, op. cit., pp. 180–1 for a fuller discussion of this point.
4. As described in, for example, Turner, H. A., Clack, G. and Roberts, G., *Labour Relations in the Motor Industry* (Cambridge, Cambridge University Press, 1967).
5. The category was introduced into the classification by cause from 1975 and it includes all types of stoppage that have no connection with the terms and conditions of work. In addition to political strikes, the category would include requests for social reforms and protests in defiance of national or international events, which can be considered quasi-political in origin (see Chapter 9 for further details).
6. ILO, *International Recommendations on Labour Statistics* (Geneva, ILO, 1976), Chapter 9: 'Industrial disputes', p. 121.
7. Fisher, M., *Measurement of Labour Disputes and their Economic Effects* (Paris, OECD, 1973), p. 59.
8. This figure is derived from the latest *New Earnings Survey* (London, DE/HMSO) carried out in April 1982. The results show that for men aged 21 and over, the average weekly hours of manual workers were 44.3 of which 4.9 were overtime hours. Corresponding figures for non-manual males were 38.2, of which only 1.2 were overtime hours. For women aged 18 and over, the overtime figures are traditionally much lower with only 1.0 hour of overtime for manual females and 0.4 for non-manual female workers.
9. Batstone, E., Boraston, I. and Frenkel, S., *The Social Organisation of Strikes* (Oxford, Basil Blackwell, 1978), p. 45.
10. In Walsh, K., 'Industrial disputes activity in some EEC countries: A regional perspective', *Manpower Studies*, No. 3 (Autumn 1981).

3   INTERNATIONAL COMPARABILITY

Any comparison of the official statistics on stoppages of work across the nine countries should be based on a thorough understanding of the differences that exist in the derived figures in each case. The differences can be rationalised into three major areas for consideration as follows:

information collection;
definitions;
measures and classifications.

These comprehensively cover the whole statistical collection and presentation exercise, from the methods of measurement through to the final publication of the details, and the three headings form the basic structure for this chapter, which concentrates on outlining the main differences.

Perhaps it would be too much to expect each of the nine countries examined here to have systems of measurement identical to each other, even if this might be considered the ideal. In most cases the methods used to collect the regular information have evolved over a fairly long period of time and reflect the particular characteristics of each country in its attitude and disposition towards disputes generally. The systems of measurement have, therefore, become entrenched, with little evidence in the nine countries of any significant change in the basic methods at least over the past decade.

This lack of change does have its advantages, of course, since it provides a degree of continuity which should ensure some reasonably accurate trend statistics on a national level. This can also be a useful asset for international comparisons since it permits fairly accurate trend comparisons if replicated across the nine countries. But with the advantages must come disadvantages, and these mainly concern the absence of change which has meant that those national systems which are particularly cumbersome or weak in operation have not been improved at all.

To some extent there has been very little external guidance available for national systems to follow. The main assistance that exists—the ILO guidelines—largely concentrate on the types of data to collect and exclude specific proposals on methodology or, for example, on what agencies could best collect information. The

ILO seemed to take the view that the mechanics of collection of the basic information was beyond their remit and would in any case arise out of existing national systems. In this they were probably correct, since time has shown that there has not been any significant change in most countries, but then this also applies to other types of economic data as well.

Information collection

The first consideration in the process of collecting the necessary information on stoppages is to have a focus, one that is known and accessible especially to the providers of the information, in most cases the employer. This focus will be of prime importance no matter what the legal requirements are in terms of the initial reporting of stoppages. For most countries the focus is provided by the relevant branch of the national Employment or Labour Department as shown in Table 3.1, which summarises the main factors to consider in assessing the comparability of the collection of information. However, there are three exceptions to this: Belgium, Italy and Denmark.

In the first two cases, Belgium and Italy, the focus for reporting is the local police force. The involvement of the police in the recording of stoppages of work arises from the largely historical perception of such action as a potential cause of civil commotion. The fact that such systems still exist despite the fairly widespread regard amongst countries that, albeit with some exceptions, strike action is a legitimate measure for workers to take, illustrates the entrenchment of the measurement systems. However, in both Belgium and Italy, though the police are involved at the notification stage, the provision of such information by employers is still in most respects voluntary.

In Denmark an altogether unique system exists, the informality of which brings into question the validity and usefulness of that country's statistics. Here the focus for reporting the incidence of stoppages is an employers' confederation, usually whichever one the employer is affiliated to, if any. But therein lies part of the problem. Some employers are not members of a confederation, particularly the smaller organisations, though this is by no means exclusively so. Thus some sectors which contain many non-confederate organisations (for example, agriculture) are effectively excluded from the statistics. More serious criticism of the Danish system, however, has to be levelled at the apparent absence of any effective measures on the part of the confederations to gather as complete a picture of the stoppage as is possible. But then why should they be expected to do so? They inevitably do this aspect of their work in a perfunctory

Table 3.1 Comparability of information collection

Information collection	Belgium	Denmark	France	Germany	Ireland	Italy	Netherlands	UK	USA
1. Agency with responsibility for gathering data	Local police	Employers' confederations	Labour inspectorate	Federal Employment Service	Dept of Labour/Central Statistics Office	Local police	Public Employment Service	Unemployment Benefit Offices	Bureau of Labor Statistics
2. Supplementary methods	Press reports	None	Press reports, nationalized industries	None	Dept of Social Welfare reports	None	Press Reports	Press reports, trade unions, nationalized industries	Press reports, trade unions, employers' associations, others
3. Agency responsible for collation and publication	Institut National de Statistique	Danmarks Statistik	Ministère du Travail	Statistisches Bundesamt	Central Statistics Office	Istituto Centrale di Statistica	Centraal Bureau Voor de Statistiek	Department of Employment	Bureau of Labor Statistics
4. Use of a standard form to gather the details	Yes	Yes	Yes	Yes	Yes	No	Yes, but not completed by employer	No	Yes, one each to the employer and union
5. Status of reporting a stoppage	Voluntary	Voluntary	Voluntary	Obligatory by law	Voluntary	Voluntary	Voluntary	Voluntary	Voluntary
6. Frequency of publication of the statistics	Monthly and annually	Annually	Monthly and annually	Annually	Quarterly and annually	Monthly and annually	Annually	Monthly and annually	Weekly, monthly and annually

manner only as far as is required for the basic information. There is little incentive to do otherwise. This significant bias to non-recording must seriously bring into question the validity of comparisons of the Danish statistics with the other eight countries.

It has already been mentioned that in Belgium and Italy the notification of disputes to the appropriate agency is voluntary, and this is also the case in the other countries, with the exception of Germany. In that country employers are obliged by law to notify the local office of the Federal Employment Service of the outbreak of a stoppage (either strike or lockout). In practice, however, it is not clear what effect this compulsion has on notification and coverage of the statistics. It would seem that this law on information provision is extremely difficult to enforce anyway, and this fact, coupled with the use of minimum size criteria for inclusion anyway, must mean that it has only a marginal effect on the total number of recorded stoppages. As Part III shows in detail, Germany has a comparatively low overall recorded level of disputes activity, so any effect from the legal requirement would inevitably be quite small.

Once the appropriate agency is aware of the outbreak of a strike or lockout (and this could be through either an employer reporting it or through the agency finding out about it from a press report, for example) the next step is to gather the details. Again, in the nine countries covered, there is no legal compulsion for employers to provide this detailed information[1] and though the meagre evidence available suggests that most employers do respond to such requests, the quality of that response in terms of completeness of detail in many cases seems to be variable.

One way to ensure that full details of a dispute are collected on a relatively consistent basis is to use a standard form which can be sent out to employers for them to complete. Of the nine countries, five send such forms to the employer for completion—Belgium, France, Germany, Ireland and the USA.[2] In the Netherlands a standard form is used, but this is filled out by the staff at the employment office on information given by the employer, while in Denmark forms are available on request at the employers' confederations to be filled out by the employer. That leaves two countries, Italy and the UK, where no forms are used and here the information is collected in a less formalised way.

The prescribed forms for each country differ in their coverage though naturally with many common points of information sought. As an example, the form currently in use in Ireland is reproduced in Figure 3.1. The value of all such forms is in their consistency and they must, therefore, be seen as a valuable aid to the information-gathering exercise. This value probably extends to international comparisons as well, since much of the information requested is of a similar range between countries, thus at least ensuring coverage of the major questions.

Collation and publication

In most of the nine countries the collation and ultimately the publication of the regular statistics on stoppages is handled by the national statistical agencies. This is the case in Belgium, Denmark, Germany, Ireland, Italy and the Netherlands, where the statistical agencies are not generally involved with the actual collection of the basic information and are distanced from the initial reporting. The reasons for this divorce of responsibility lie in historical precedent, especially where the national statistical offices are, after all, the best equipped to handle the data and frequently include the results in the much broader range of statistical information produced by them. Thus statistics on strikes appear alongside other economic variables such as unemployment or output, for example.

However, in a number of cases, the separation of the responsibilities of collection and publication of the details is deliberate policy. In some countries there was a perceived need to keep the publication of the details of strikes and lockouts in the hands of a visibly impartial agency, not involved with other aspects of particular disputes. For example, the national labour department, often used as the focus for information collection, may also be involved with administering labour law or setting up arbitration for the very disputes that statistics were being gathered on. In such circumstances it is possible that some users and commentators on the statistics might question the quality of the data published if the statistical agency was the same as that administering the dispute.

It is difficult to say how much this consideration is relevant today. Certainly in the past the concern to have a separation of the recording of the stoppages from the publication of the details has been the underlying reason for the separation of the tasks in, for example, Italy and Germany, though this is likely to be a less contentious issue today. However, the system has become the accepted practice and remains so at present.

In the three remaining countries of France, the UK and the USA, the respective ministries of labour are responsible for both the collation and publication of the information. In all three cases the data collation is carried out by the statistical branches or sub-departments

AN ROINN LEASA SHÓISIALAIGH

OIFIG AITIÚIL.............................

TO: ....

NOTIFICATION OF A TRADE DISPUTE

As soon as a trade dispute occurs, or is known to be pending, or has ceased, particulars in regard thereto should be entered below and copies of the completed form despatched in envelopes marked "*Trade Dispute*" to:—

(*a*) The Director, Central Statistics Office, Dublin 2.

(*b*) The Secretary, Department of Labour, Mespil Road, Dublin 4.

(*c*) The Secretary, Department of Social Welfare, U.B. Decisions, Section, 157/164 Townsend St., Dublin 2.

(*d*) The Registrar, The Labour Court, Department of Labour, Mespil Road, Dublin 4.

(*e*) The Secretary, Department of Social Welfare, Disability Benefit Section, Aras Mhic Dhiarmada, Dublin 1.

Information should be given as fully as possible under the heads set out. State at (3), not only the names of the parties directly concerned, but the name of the Trade Union (with address of the Local Secretary) at (a) and the name of the Employers' Association at (b) if either or both these bodies are involved. If the dispute arises out of a claim for an increase of wages and/or a reduction of working hours, the wages and hours obtaining at the time of the dispute should be stated at (13). If the dispute results in any alteration in wages and/or hours, the new wages and/or hours should be stated at (15). In addition, the usual report should be furnished on Form S.11.

It is of the utmost importance that paragraph 16 of this form be completed in all cases, and that action be taken as directed therein.

(1) Locality and Town ... ...

(2) Trade and Occupation affected ... ...

(3) Names and addresses of Parties affected:—

    (*a*) ....

                    v.

    (*b*) ....

(4) Duration of normal working week (five or six days). ....

(5) Number of firms (employers) involved ... .

(6) Approx. number of workers involved

    (*a*) Directly ... ...

    (*b*) Indirectly ... ...

(7) (a) Date and time (approx.) on which work ceased ... ...

    (b) Was the stoppage of work "official"? ....

(8) Date on which work was resumed ... .

(9) Was the work on which the dispute occurred "Work under an Employment Scheme"? ... ...

(10) Date and source of information ... ...

(11) Orders in circulation (if any) affected and the circulation of which has been suspended ... ...

(12) Cause of Dispute ... ...

(13) Particulars of demand made by either party or both ... ...

(14) If settled, whether settlement was arrived at by direct negotiation or otherwise ... .

(15) Actual terms of settlement ... ...

S. 13. [P.T.O.

Figure 3.1 The data collection form used in Ireland

REMARKS:

....
....
....
....
....
....
....
....
....
....
....
....
....
....
....
....
....
....
....
....
....
....
....
....
....

(16) The Secretary of the Trade Union concerned was asked on.................................(Date), to
inform the workers involved of their right to furnish evidence of unemployment for credit
purposes for the duration of the Trade dispute.

....

Signed—	Rank—	Date—

(540)125530. 10,000. 9-78. F.P.—G30.

of the labour ministry as a well established practice, though clearly
the production of statistics on stoppages covers only a small part of
their overall work.

As Table 3.1 (line 2) shows, some of the nine countries use supplementary sources of information to support that received through the
normal channel. In most cases this takes the form of a scan of press
reports by the publishing agency to see if any reported disputes
have escaped the normal notification processes. Such reports can
also provide extra information on stoppages that the agency is
already aware of, though perhaps in only limited detail. The use
of press reports is one of the major sources of information used by
the US Bureau of Labor Statistics in compiling its regular series
(see Chapter 12), though in other countries such as Belgium, France
and the UK, such accounts generally only provide a relatively minor
input to the total picture.

Recent results published by the Netherlands central statistical
agency, the CBS, provides an indication of how valuable the press
coverage of stoppages over the period 1970–80 is.[3] The data (more
fully explored in Chapter 10) isolated those reported stoppages
which escaped inclusion into the official statistics. Over this eleven-
year period they discovered that approximately 18 per cent of all
stoppages occurring were not recorded. However, most of these
were of fairly short duration (though the Netherlands does not have
a minimum size for inclusion) and in total only accounted for
about 2 per cent of the revised total of working days lost. So, at
least in the case of the Netherlands, it would seem that the extra
information provided by press reports has only a limited value,
and the coverage of the regular methods of collection may be considered good.

In addition to the use of press reports for supplementary information, three of the nine countries, France, the UK and the USA,
make use of direct information supplied by state industry or trade
unions, for example. In the case of the USA, the use of these alternative sources of information is relied on more as an extra input to
complete the whole picture. In practice, however, the amount of
data coming from such sources is both variable and limited. For
example, the amount of information provided by trade unions in
the USA is very limited, since they tend not to respond to requests
for information by the BLS. This is also true at the level of the
trade union confederations.

In France and the UK though, these supplementary sources are
better established to such an extent that they can be relied on for useful, accurate and consistent data. In particular, the state industries

such as coal mining in the UK or the railways in France keep good records of their own industrial disputes and at the same time have a relatively active strike record. Therefore, this information can be made available to the appropriate agencies for inclusion in the overall statistics but with the minimum of effort on the part of that agency.

In all countries the gathering of information is a continuous process which is pulled together at regular intervals for publication. Therefore the resultant statistics should reflect the true circumstances of the dispute at the time it occurred even if it is some months later that the details are published. In general too, the methods of collection and the agencies used for the purpose do not show wide differences amongst the nine countries. The more subtle differences, to be found in the use of supplementary sources of information by six of the countries, may mean that those who do not use similar additional sources (in the case of Denmark, Germany and Italy) may as a result miss out some of the smaller disputes which are less easy to detect by the conventional methods. However, discrepancies because of this will greatly depend on what measure of activity is being used, with the number of stoppages being the most affected and working time lost the least.

Definitions

The validity of international comparisons of data on stoppages of work will depend ultimately on the coverage of the statistics collected by each country, or in other words a combination of what is included or excluded. The treatment of various types of stoppage, for example those of a political nature, or the treatment of certain effects such as indirect effects, will control the overall coverage of the statistics and so an understanding of these differences will enable the statistics to be used with any necessary qualifications applied to them.

Unfortunately there are a great many caveats to be attached to the use of the statistics across the nine countries examined here. Table 3.2 summarises ten of the major considerations in matrix form, and, though there are more than these factors to take into account they are generally of less importance to the comparability issue. As the table shows, there are some common approaches to various definitions, but equally there are some wide differences in the treatment of some fundamental issues which can cause serious reservations in any international comparison of the statistics.

Table 3.2 Comparability of definitions

Definitions	Belgium	Denmark	France	Germany	Ireland	Italy	Netherlands	UK	USA
1. Minimum size for inclusion	<One working day	<100 working days lost	None	<One working day <10 workers or <100 working days lost	<One working day or <10 working days lost	None	None	<One working day or <10 workers or <100 working days lost	<One working day or <6 workers (From Jan. 1982: <1,000 workers)
2. Reporting unit	Place where dispute first occurred	Local establishment	Local unit	Local unit	Local unit	Enterprise level	Local unit where dispute first occurs	Local unit	Local unit
3. Lockouts	Included	Included	Included	Included	Included	Included	Included	Included	Included
4. Indirect effects	Measured	Measured	Not measured	Not measured	Measured	Not measured	Measured	Measured	Measured

5. Secondary effects	Not measured	Not measured	Not measured	Not measured	Not measured	Not measured	Not measured	Not measured	Not measured
6. Official and unofficial action	Both included	Both included	Both included	Both included	Both included	Both included	Both included	Both included	Both included
7. Sympathetic action	Mostly included	Included	Included	Included	Included	Included	Included	Included	Included
8. Political protest stoppages	Not included	Included	Not included	Included	Included	Included	Included	Not included	Not included
9. Excluded sectors	None	Non-members of an employers' confederation	Agriculture, public admin.	None	None	None	None	None	None
10. Excluded occupational groups	Police, armed forces	Police, armed forces, others	Police, armed forces, others	Police, armed forces, others	Police, armed forces	Military personnel	Police, armed forces, others	Police, armed forces	Police, armed forces, others

Minimum size

The most obvious difference in the definitions applied to the statistics in each country is most apparent at the recording stage.[4] This is the application of a minimum size to disputes, with those falling under the threshold excluded from the statistics. The rationale for having such an exclusion rule has already been discussed fully in Chapter 2, but hinges mainly on the desire to limit the amount of data collection necessary by excluding the smallest stoppages and establishments affected. As a result, the number of stoppages will be seriously underestimated but there will be less effect on the other two measures of workers involved and working days lost.

As a result, of the nine countries covered, six have such a minimum size criterion, while the remaining three have none and in theory include all these stoppages coming to the notice of the recording agency. But looking at the six countries that do have such minima in more detail, there are five different criteria between them. Two countries, Germany and the UK, have a common definition with those stoppages lasting less than one working day or involving less than ten workers excluded from the statistics except where the aggregate of working days lost exceeds 100.[5] However, in the remaining four countries the definitions are all different. In Belgium, for example, those stoppages lasting less than one working day are excluded. In Ireland the same criterion applies and also stoppages involving less than ten working days are excluded. In the USA, up to the end of 1981, the definition had a similar alternative measure of size but only those involving less than six workers were excluded. Since the beginning of 1982, however, the criterion has been changed and, as a result, the coverage of the statistics has drastically narrowed to include only those involving 1,000 or more workers, thus making this the most restrictive definition of the nine countries. Prior to 1982, the most restrictive definition was that for Denmark where all those stoppages involving less than 100 working days lost were excluded.

The use of a minimum size for inclusion would not be such an impediment to international comparisons if each country used the same criterion. However, as has been demonstrated, only two of the six have the same one. In addition, three countries include stoppages of all sizes, further complicating comparisons between the nine. In short, therefore, these differences will seriously affect the coverage of all measures of activity, though on the basis that the majority of working time lost during a period is attributable to a small number of large stoppages, the measure of working time lost will be affected proportionately less than others.

Reporting unit

The nine countries have similar rules about the point of focus for the reporting of a stoppage. This is taken to be the local unit or establishment at which the dispute first occurs, though with some variation in how the unit is defined evident in some of the countries, as shown in Table 3.2. Taking the local unit as the focus means that all information on the dispute, including, for example, sending a form requesting the specific details, will be aimed at this level. In those multi-plant organisations, therefore, direct reference is not made to the corporate headquarters, though the local unit may involve head office at some stage, particularly if, say, the industrial relations function is carried out at a headquarters level as opposed to being plant-based.

In those cases where a dispute with a common cause or starting point affects a number of establishments within one organisation, then all countries appear to approach the collection of information in a similar way. Each individual district unit would be approached individually for information, but would, of course, be treated appropriately in the main measures of activity, such as number of stoppages and number of establishments affected.

Types of action

The various types of action that can take place, or some effects of this action, provide an important key to the comparability of the data across the nine countries. Dealing with the similarities first, all nine countries treat lockouts, secondary effects, official and unofficial action and sympathetic action in the same way. Lockouts are included in the statistics, though in most of the nine countries their occurrence is thought to be rare. However, since only one country, Germany, actually publishes separate details of strikes and lockouts it is difficult to be more precise on their incidence.

Similarly, official and unofficial action is counted in all countries, so the level or degree of trade union involvement does not affect the measurement of a dispute. Sympathetic action is also counted in the statistics of each country, irrespective of the legal status of such action. For all such action, though, the presentation of separate statistics on each is variable with the majority of countries choosing not to show separate statistics.

In the case of any secondary effects, specifically those at an establishment different from the one where the dispute occurs, none of the nine countries make any attempt to measure such action. Of itself this is an omission which makes the data series deficient by an unknown but probably significant quantity. Yet from the point of view of international comparisons of the statistics, because all countries exclude such effects comparisons are not jeopardised. In any case, as has already been explained in Chapter 2, effective measurement of such secondary effects would be extremely difficult since in only a few cases would the extent of layoffs at other establishments be reasonably clear for statistical purposes.

Of the remaining types of action listed in Table 3.2, that is indirect effects and political strikes, there are inconsistencies in their treatment by the nine countries which seriously affect the validity of international comparisons using some of the measures of activity.

Taking indirect effects first, out of the nine countries, six of them—Belgium, Denmark, Ireland, the Netherlands, the UK and the USA—measure and include such effects, while the remaining three countries—France, Germany and Italy—exclude these effects from their statistics. Obviously the extent of indirect effects will vary from country to country and will depend to a great extent on the particular types of stoppage experienced during a period, identified in such factors as industries affected and the duration of the disputes. For example, there is a stronger likelihood of indirect effects in a stoppage in a continuous production industry, where most of the functions within the plant (such as maintenance and stores, for example) are interdependent, especially if reaching a settlement takes a long time. Unfortunately, because only one country, the UK, actually publishes details of indirect effects separately, it is impossible to determine the extent of similar effects in the other non-measuring countries.

In the UK over the ten-year period 1972–81, the number of workers assessed as being indirectly involved in all stoppages amounted to 19.5 per cent of all workers involved (directly and indirectly) and it may be fair to assume that the three countries not measuring such effects would render similar proportions. If this is so, then clearly the effect on the two main measures of activity of workers involved and man-days lost would be considerable. Man-days lost less so, since the indirectly affected workers are usually forced to stop work only after the stoppage has begun to affect production. Obviously the other two main measures of activity, the number of stoppages and establishments involved, would not be affected by the exclusion of indirect effects. Therefore, in comparisons with the other countries, using the first two measures of activity, the statistics for France, Germany and Italy must be considered underestimates.

In the case of France, the degree of underestimation is also aggravated by the exclusion of political strikes from the statistics. In addition to France, three other countries, Belgium, the UK and the USA also exclude political stoppages where they can be identified as such. Again in the absence of comprehensive statistics on the extent of political stoppages in the remaining countries that do include them, and given the definitional problems, the example of one country is taken to show the possible extent of such action.

Chapter 2 reported that the extent of political protest stoppages in Italy over the period 1975–80 accounted for approximately 21 per cent of all working time lost. This is a high figure and one which is perhaps untypical of the other countries where the use of political strikes is more limited than in Italy's case. However, there is no doubt that in those countries where such action is considered legitimate (and only Germany specifically outlaws such action) the political stoppages could account for a significant proportion of all main measures of activity with the possible exception of the number of stoppages.[6] As such, in the four countries which exclude such action, the overall statistics will again contribute to underestimation.

Excluded sectors and groups

In two of the nine countries, France and Denmark, the statistics suffer from the exclusion of certain industrial sectors to such an extent that international comparability may be affected. In the case of France the exclusions are relatively straightforward. In that country, the statistics do not take into account the sectors of agriculture and public administration, the latter at both a local and national level. The reasons why these two groups are excluded are not at all clear, though it would seem that it is mainly for historical reasons and to a lesser extent due to the perceived low incidence of stoppages in these particular sectors. Certainly in agriculture the incidence of industrial disputes is probably very low, based on the experience of other countries, but this may not be the case with the public administration sector, and the exclusion in this case must seriously affect the value of the aggregated data.

The second country to exclude certain sectors, Denmark, does so by virtue of its measurement system. Because the main agencies used for recording disputes are the employers' federations, then those sectors of industry with a low incidence of such affiliation will tend not to be recorded. In the main this will affect such sectors as agriculture as well as those sectors where the normal business unit is comparatively small as measured in numbers employed. In practice, however, the incidence of stoppages of work in the smaller businesses will tend to be small anyway and so the net effect on the four main measures of activity should only be a small degree of underestimation. Furthermore, given the Danish minimum size for recording a stoppage of less than 100 working days lost, it is probable that most such disputes would fall below this threshold anyway.

Though the majority of the nine countries do not exclude specific sectors of industry from the statistics, all nine do concur in their treatment of the police and armed forces personnel who are effectively excluded from the statistics, through the fact that these occupational groups are prohibited from taking strike action. This prohibition is usually couched in terms which indirectly refer to strike action. For example, the terms of employment may include a reference to the fact that they must be subject to the discipline of the force, and clearly a strike could be construed as a breach of discipline. In some countries, the police and armed forces are still free to join a trade union even if their choice to strike is curtailed.

Apart from the police and armed forces, in five of the countries further occupational groups are effectively excluded from the statistics. In Denmark and Germany, for example, certain higher level government workers receive security of tenure in their jobs in return for a non-strike clause in their contracts of employment. In France, the Netherlands and the USA, the restrictions on striking tend to apply to groups of government employees considered to be in key jobs which, if they took strike action, might jeopardise public safety. These would include air traffic controllers, for example. In the remaining four countries, there are no similar exclusions to consider, though there might be some isolated cases of no-strike agreements being organised.

The effect of no-strike clauses in the contracts of employment of certain government employees effectively rules out the possibilities of strike action from these groups in most cases. In terms of the statistics, this means that there will be differences in the comparative size of the labour forces that could potentially take strike action, which might account for some of the observed variation in stoppage activity between the countries (more fully explored in Part III). The problem is that it is impossible to quantify the potential effect on the statistics, since at any one time it will be dependent on a whole series of factors all of which play their part in creating a strike. The easy option is to assume that the effect will on the whole be negligible.

Measures and classifications

The third major area of comparability concerns the nature of the available information on stoppages in terms of the main measures of activity and classifications of them. International comparisons of the statistics are really only possible where there are similar ranges of information available to compare, after which the qualifications which arise out of the discrepancies in both collection methods and the definitions applied can be brought into the analysis. The coverage by each country is summarised in the matrix in Table 3.3.

Main measures

All nine countries regularly produce statistics on the two main measures of number of workers involved and working time lost (days lost in all countries except Italy, where the measure is working hours lost). Also, all of the countries except Germany use the measure of number of stoppages, and a further four—Belgium, France, Germany and Ireland—add the number of establishments affected. It is therefore, possible to use the statistics produced by each country to compare stoppage activity in its broadest terms, ignoring for the moment any definitional problems which affect such comparisons and which must be raised later.

Classifications

However, the main measures of activity provide only the basic amount of detail for international comparisons, but all countries produce in varying amounts some classifications of these main measures and thus provide the essential details for a better understanding of the types and nature of stoppages being experienced in each country.

As Table 3.3 illustrates, the country hitherto producing most of the classifications of its data was the USA. However, that was before the rationalisation of its statistical coverage of industrial disputes which took effect from 1982 (described more fully in Chapter 12), since when the output has been seriously curtailed. The least amount of detail published is that by Denmark, with just one classification by industries affected. The large differences in the coverage of each country cause severe problems in international comparisons using the nine countries, though the potential is obviously increased if only a limited number of countries is used, basically those producing a similar range of classifications.

In fact, the only classification common to all nine countries is that by industries affected, but even here there is the added problem

Table 3.3 Comparability of main measures and classifications of activity

Measure/classification	Country								
	Belgium	Denmark	France	Germany	Ireland	Italy	Netherlands	UK	USA
Main measures									
1. Number of stoppages	X	X	X		X	X	X	X	X
2. Establishments affected	X		X	X	X		X		X
3. Workers involved	X	X	X	X	X	X	X	X	X
4. Working time lost*	X	X	X	X	X	X	X	X	X
Classifications									
1. Cause	X				X	X	X	X	X
2. Industries affected	X	X	X	X	X	X	X	X	X
3. Occupations affected								X	X
4. Regions	X		X	X		X	X	X	X
5. Duration	X			X	X		X	X	X
6. Size of establishment	X								
7. Importance of disputes					X	X		X	X
8. Principal disputes								X	X
9. Method of settlement						X	X		X
10. Contractual status									X
11. Trade union involved					X			X	X

*Working days lost in all countries except Italy where working hours are used instead.

of each country using its own particular industrial classification which, in terms of specific industry detail, can vary considerably. This is amply illustrated by reference to the appropriate tables in the national chapters in Part II, where those covering working days lost by industry generally use the groupings normally published.

Seven of the nine countries publish a classification of the main measures by regions, but this is less useful in international comparisons given the large regional differences in both size and industrial structure which must be taken into account to get meaningful results. All the seven countries except France limit the regional analyses to the standard planning regions (the fifty states plus the District of Columbia in the USA). In France, details are regularly published for each of the smaller *départements* and this is the best level of disaggregation of all the nine countries.

Six countries also produce analyses by the duration of stoppages, though in fact information must be available in the other three countries, Denmark, France, and Italy, though it is not published, since this information is essential in order to calculate the amount of working time lost (together with workers involved).

The ostensible cause of the recorded disputes is reported by only six of the nine countries, but international comparability is not helped by the use of different categories of cause in each country. As a result, only the broadest of comparisons are possible using this classification despite its undoubted importance in understanding the nature of stoppage activity. Of the six countries that do publish details by cause, Belgium has the most comprehensive set of categories (see Chapter 4). The potential for international comparisons by cause is discussed further in Chapter 14, with some limited comparisons.

For the remaining classifications listed in Table 3.3, such as those by occupations affected and method of settlement, for example, the coverage in terms of the number of countries regularly producing them is small. The classification by occupations affected, for example, is only attempted by three of the nine countries and in these three cases (Ireland, the UK and the USA) the coverage is limited, no doubt to some extent reflecting the difficulties in defining occupations in a suitably succinct form. A selection of the main classifications form the basis of some of the chapters covered later in Part III.

Conclusion

The sometimes significant differences to be found in both the methods of collection of the basic information and the definitions applied to the statistics on stoppages do put into question the validity of international comparisons of the data. The variations in data collection will to some extent affect the coverage of all disputes, but the problem is particularly pronounced in the case of Denmark. In that country the system is much more casual than in the remaining eight countries which must limit the proportion of all stoppages actually recorded.

However, the most serious limits to comparability arise out of the different definitions applied to the statistics and in particular the use of a minimum size for exclusion in the main series. Using a minimum size is not the questionable factor *per se*, but more the fact that some countries choose not to use one. This largely affects the main measures of number of stoppages and establishments involved, and to a lesser extent the number of workers involved, rather than the measure of working time lost. This is because the majority of working time lost during a period is attributable to a small number of large stoppages (see Table 2.4, for example) which would tend not to be affected by any minimum size criteria.

Despite this, the amount of working time lost will be affected by the differing treatment of both indirect effects and political stoppages in particular, with those countries which exclude such effects seriously underestimating the amount of both workers involved and time lost. The other measures of number of stoppages and establishments involved will be less affected by these exclusions. Of the nine France is perhaps the worst case since in that country both indirect effects and political stoppages are excluded, resulting in potentially serious underestimation when compared to most of the other eight countries.

In many ways the amount of attention given to the statistics and reflected in the range of published information available is very much a function of the past record of stoppage activity in each country. Part III shows more fully that countries such as the UK and the USA exhibit some of the highest recorded activity in industrial disputes over the past decade and these countries in particular produce at the same time the widest range of information. The question arises, however, does the existence of a reasonably comprehensive recording mechanism engender the interest? In other words, a good system of measurement will show a fuller and probably more extensive stoppage record than an essentially casual system which may not pick up many of the stoppages that occur. As a result there will be more interest in the statistics and a realisation that they are fairly accurate in what they are attempting to measure.

In all the countries the methods of measurement have been in continuous operation for long periods with only the minimum of changes. This means that within each country the national statistics can provide reasonably accurate trend statistics going back in most cases beyond the decade covered in this study. Therefore, international comparisons of these trends should be the least problematic in any attempt to compare the statistics across countries, but this inevitably limits the amount of useful analyses that can be made.

For more detailed cross-sectional comparisons the problems are legion. No two countries of the nine can be said to be compiling their statistics on exactly similar lines. However, there are clearly identifiable groups of countries within the nine where such comparisons should be more acceptable within clearly defined limits. One group consists of Ireland, the UK and the USA, for example, where the definitions of inclusion criteria show only minor differences. Belgium could be added to the list possibly, though its minimum for inclusion of less than one working day is more restrictive than the other three (see Table 3.2).

The temptation to compare the recorded stoppages activity between the nine countries is too great, however, and Part III explores some of the main aspects that can be compared with some success. In all such comparisons though, there is always the qualification that each country measures its stoppages in different ways. It should also be remembered that the record in each country will be greatly influenced, *inter alia*, by the general atmosphere in each country towards strikes and lockouts. This atmosphere will be reflected in such factors as the effect of trade unions and industrial relations practices in each country, and the substance of Chapter 16 is devoted to a discussion of these specific points.

Notes

1. Outside the nine countries covered in this study there is evidence of different legal conditions. For example, in Australia employers are required by law to supply full details of any stoppage occurring at their establishment at the request of the collection agency. Reported in Creigh, S., Donaldson, N. and Hawthorn, E., 'Stoppage activity in OECD countries', *Employment Gazette* (November 1980), pp. 1174-81.
2. In the USA the Bureau of Labor Statistics actually sends out two forms simultaneously, one to the employer and one to the trade union involved.
3. As published in *Sociale Maandstatistiek*, CBS, (June 1982). Further details of this special analysis are discussed in Chapter 10.
4. Though in most countries the minimum size criteria are applied *before* the details of the stoppage are gathered, there will be cases where the full details are sent to the collection agency and only then is the exclusion applied. In

such cases details of the smaller disputes, not normally published, may be available in an unpublished form.

5. The two countries have this common minimum size definition because Germany followed the UK's example after the end of the 1939–45 war.

6. In the UK, for example, the latest figures for 1981 excluded stoppages of work by fishermen in February, gas workers in July and car industry workers in October, all protesting about the lack of Government response on a particular issue, or making a wider protest not directly concerned with the terms and conditions of employment. In all, these three stoppages involved around 111,000 workers but were not included in the official statistics. For more details see 'Stoppages caused by industrial disputes in 1981', *Employment Gazette* (July 1982).

PART II

NATIONAL STATISTICS

4 BELGIUM

Method of measurement

In Belgium, though there is no specific law covering the point, the occurrence of an industrial dispute is supposed to be communicated to the local police (at the level of the Commune) by the employer, though in many cases the police may discover the dispute before a formal communication is received. The police pass the information about disputes in their particular area on to the Ministry of Employment and Labour (Ministère de l'Emploi et du Travail) and to the National Statistical Institute (Institut National de Statistique—INS). It is the latter organisation, the INS, which has responsibility for following up the initial notifications.

On hearing of the outbreak of a dispute, the INS responds by sending a detailed questionnaire to the employer to gather the full details of the stoppage. Usually it is completed when the dispute has been resolved and normal working resumed, but in the case of a protracted dispute a completed form might be returned during the course of the stoppage and at the end. The gathering of this information is a continuous process, though the regular statistics are only compiled on a monthly basis.

In an effort to avoid missing any stoppages that might not have come to the attention of the police, the INS supplements this primary source of information with various *ad hoc* measures, including scanning press reports, for example, in an effort to cover as many disputes as possible. The scanning may also provide further details on disputes that the INS already knows about but has failed to get complete information on from the employer.

Definitions

Conditions for inclusion

All stoppages coming to the attention of the INS are included in the statistics, except those which last less than one working day. This exclusion is much a reflection of the difficulties to be encountered in measuring the very small disputes which start and finish in a short period of time, especially given the system of measurement in Belgium, depending as it does on questionnaires being sent out and returned.

Definition of establishment

The reporting unit for gathering the information is taken to be the location at which the dispute first broke out. Even where a number of separate establishments experienced a stoppage at the same time and over the same issue, each would normally be required to provide details of their particular stoppage. However, in such instances they would be counted as one stoppage, whereas they would be counted separately in the measure of the number of establishments involved (see Table 4.1).

Lockouts

If a lockout occurs, then this would be included in the statistics though not distinguished separately from strikes. Where a strike and a lockout occur simultaneously at the same establishment, only one stoppage would be recorded.

Indirect effects

The indirect effects of a stoppage to workers at the same establishment would be included in the measures number of workers involved and working days lost. Numbers indirectly affected (*chômeurs forcés*) are given separately in the regular statistics.

Secondary effects

Any secondary effects at establishments other than that where the stoppage broke out are not measured.

Official/unofficial disputes

Both official and unofficial disputes are included in the regular statistics but they are not shown separately. One of the categories of cause of stoppage covers 'trade union matters' but is not strictly an indication of the degree of union involvement in a dispute, more it is those disputes concerned with union issues such as recognition, time-off for union duties, and other similar ones.

Sympathetic action

Any sympathetic action taken by workers either in an existing establishment experiencing a stoppage or at a separate one is included in the statistics. Such action can also be identified separately in the analysis by cause of stoppage under 'solidarity strikes' (see Table 4.4—sympathetic action).

Political strikes

Any stoppages with an identifiable political motive are excluded from the statistics. In any case most action of this sort is usually of very short duration, such as a mass stoppage for few hours, and so would automatically be excluded from the statistics by application of the minimum size criterion of less than one working day in duration.

Excluded sectors or groups

There are no specific sectors of industry excluded from the statistics and the only occupational groups prohibited to take strike action are the police and the armed forces.

Measures and classifications

The following main measures of activity are regularly used in the statistics:

    number of stoppages;
    number of establishments involved;
    number of workers involved;
    number of working days lost.

Those stoppages simultaneously affecting a number of different establishments but with an identified common cause, would be counted as one stoppage in the number of stoppages measure, but in multiple for the number of establishments involved. The number of workers involved is usually taken to be the average numbers both directly and indirectly affected during the course of the stoppage.

Cause

The classification by cause is relatively comprehensive and normally uses seven main categories as follows: (1) Salary/wage issues; (2) bonus, social allowances, compensation issues; (3) working conditions; (4) employment problems (distinct from working conditions and would include such issues as redundancy or the contraction of the business); (5) trade union matters; (6) sympathetic action; and (7) other causes. More specific details of cause are listed as necessary under each of these broad headings.

Industry

Ten broad groupings of industries are usually employed in the published statistics as follows: (1) agriculture, forestry and fishing; (2) energy and water; (3) chemical production; (4) engineering; (5) other manufacturing industries; (6) building and civil engineering; (7) commerce, repairs and restoration; (8) transport and communications; (9) banking, insurance, finance and business services; (10) other services. In addition these broad groups are further broken down into approximately thirty-one smaller groups under each of the broader headings shown above.

Region

The statistics for the number of workers directly involved only are regularly published by the nine Belgian provinces of: Anvers; Brabant; Hainaut; Liège; Limbourg; Luxembourg; Namur; East Flanders; and West Flanders.

Duration

The duration of stoppages is divided into eleven bands measured in days, from the smallest category of less than two days (and in effect more than one, since stoppages lasting less than one day are excluded) to the largest of eighty-one days and over.

Size of establishment

The size of establishment is measured in numbers of workers from less than five, through seven further divisions until the largest of 1,000 workers or more.

Cross-classifications

There are no cross-classifications of the main single classifications regularly published, though there may be additional information available from the INS that is not published (including the possibility of basic details of stoppages lasting less than one working day).

Availability of the information

The monthly figures on stoppages are first released through a monthly press release or *Communiqué Mensuel* by the INS, followed by the consolidated statistics for a longer period published in the monthly *Bulletin de Statistique*.

The most detailed source of information on stoppages (as well as most other subjects) is, however, the *Annuaire Statistique de la Belgique* which is the only source of many of the published classifications such as those by industry and province, for example.

Table 4.1 Belgium Summary statistics

	1972	1973	1974	1975	1976	1977	1978	1979	1980
Number of disputes	191	172	235	243	281	220	195	215	125
Number of firms involved	2,438	180	271	817	319	220	225	228	134
Number of workers involved	70,570	70,134	60,764	90,159	117,800	74,217	101,703	61,844	30,166
– of which directly involved	66,622	62,281	55,747	85,801	106,654	65,761	90,813	55,722	26,727
– of which indirectly involved	3,948	7,853	5,017	4,358	11,146	8,456	10,890	6,122	3,439
Number of working days lost	354,086	871,872	580,032	607,809	896,805	664,236	1,002,489	615,484	216,754

Source: Annuaire Statistique de la Belgique, Bulletin de Statistique, Institut National de Statistique.

Table 4.2 Belgium Workers directly involved by province

Province	1972*	1973*	1974*	1975*	1976*	1977	1978	1979	1980
Anvers	6,734	6,013	4,666	6,244	8,038	2,935	11,225	3,314	2,774
Brabant	8,835	2,785	6,087	9,003	4,446	3,873	10,749	6,588	1,834
Hainaut	31,849	17,049	18,121	26,505	37,553	21,681	22,844	20,072	6,111
Liège	7,315	20,039	8,034	20,595	33,052	25,825	30,986	3,908	6,525
Limbourg	2,351	5,472	7,094	1,335	5,378	2,421	8,487	13,155	2,974
Luxembourg	24	501	–	109	1,050	1,799	30	–	–
Namur	1,184	637	774	1,361	1,837	949	1,411	2,905	2,011
East Flanders	5,562	3,533	3,604	4,730	10,500	2,761	4,536	4,460	1,959
West Flanders	2,768	6,252	7,367	15,919	4,800	3,517	545	1,320	2,539
Belgium	66,622	62,281	55,747	85,801	106,654	65,761	90,813	55,722	26,727

*These figures exclude certain prominent stoppages during the year.
Source: *Annuaire Statistique de la Belgique*, Institut National de Statistique.

Table 4.3 Belgium Working days lost by industry

Industry	1972	1973	1974	1975	1976	1977	1978	1979	1980
1. Agriculture, forestry, fishing	–	900	–	391	–	–	–	–	–
2. Energy and water	9,368	19,122	39,618	32,140	32,263	27,222	32,477	89,829	8,231
3. Chemical production	128,846	338,481	148,332	91,795	513,872	206,419	449,260	65,540	81,806
4. Engineering	144,038	437,015	306,009	262,414	286,947	385,603	469,230	405,714	92,380
5. Other manufacturing industries	26,253	59,233	74,530	169,508	54,658	25,329	16,452	36,595	25,424
6. Building and civil engineering	243	200	741	681	2,162	7,680	171	2,389	89
7. Commerce, repairs and restoration	198	838	2,045	11,079	1,116	4,709	3,621	7,614	3,396
8. Transport and communications	896	34	5,138	877	217	5,090	18,057	1,643	–
9. Banking, insurance, finance and business services	42,345	368	673	–	3,162	530	–	–	2,396
10. Other services	1,899	15,681	2,946	38,924	2,408	1,654	13,221	6,160	3,032
All industries and services	354,086	871,872	580,032	607,809	896,805	664,236	1,002,489	615,484	216,754

Source: Annuaire Statistique de la Belgique, Institut National de Statistique.

Table 4.4 Belgium Working days lost by cause

	1972	1973	1974	1975	1976	1977	1978	1979	1980†
1. Salary/wages	292,310	675,607	465,447	462,640	285,449	465,374	111,860	113,313	59,688
2. Bonus, social allowance, compensation	23,018	64,058	17,449	14,114	331,705	25,474	28,341	13,607	1,174
3. Working conditions	4,957	37,777	14,563	9,600	12,622	9,354	102,531	19,000	16,287
4. Employment problems	14,063	81,925	64,676	90,729	137,446	93,598	40,444	76,622	30,833
5. Trade union matters	5,194	686	757	1,129	–	–	660,845	*	*
6. Sympathetic action	367	5,992	444	13,862	18,159	16,068	7,845	*	*
7. Other causes	14,177	5,827	16,696	15,735	111,424	54,368	50,623	392,942	108,772
All causes	354,086	871,872	580,032	607,809	896,805	664,236	1,002,489	615,484	216,754

* Included in 'other causes'.
† First eleven months only.
Source: Annuaire Statistique de la Belgique, Institut National de Statistique.

5 DENMARK

Method of measurement

The regular statistics on stoppages of work in Denmark are derived from information provided by employers to the various employers' associations on a voluntary basis. The statistical series has been continuous since 1897. The main recipient of such information is the largest of the associations, the Danish Employers' Confederation (Dansk Abejdsgiverforening), but in addition there are many smaller associations covering particular specialised sectors of industry or commerce. Information is sent to the appropriate employers' association on a continuous basis, using a special questionnaire, which is provided to the employer through the associations.

Once a year the employers' associations collect together the notifications from member companies and forward them on to the Danish central statistics agency, Danmarks Statistik (DS). Neither the employers' associations nor the statistical office become involved with chasing-up incomplete information. The statistical office remains independent of the source of the data and the employers' associations simply act as a point of contact should the employing organisation experiencing a stoppage wish to inform its representative body. The overall measurement system is characteristically informal.

This casual system of recording stoppages must mean that many are not recorded, though in the absence of alternative information it is difficult to estimate the magnitude of this under-recording. Employers frequently show a reluctance to divulge information on what is basically seen as an internal matter unless they are asked for the information specifically. In Denmark, therefore, the whole system of information collection on stoppages is geared to employers offering information voluntarily.

Definitions

Conditions for inclusions

In Denmark, all those stoppages resulting in less than 100 working days lost in total are excluded from the statistics. The method of recording does mean, however, that information on the very small

stoppages may be supplied by the employing establishments experiencing them and so may be available at the employers' associations. However, it should be noted that the associations do not
publish their own series of statistics on stoppages.

Definition of establishment

The single establishment at which the stoppage first began is taken
to be the reference point and will be the reporting unit in most
cases, supplying the information directly to the appropriate employers' association.

Lockouts

Lockouts are included in the statistics though they are not identified
separately. In practice, however, they are thought to be rare, especially in comparison to the volume of strikes.

Indirect effects

Any information on indirect effects experienced at the striking
establishment and notified by the employer to one of the employers'
associations would be counted. The information is not separately
identified in the statistics, however.

Secondary effects

Neither the employers' associations nor the statistical office make
efforts to measure any secondary effects of industrial action, though
they acknowledge its significance in any assessment of the effects
of stoppages.

Official/unofficial disputes

All information notified to the employers' associations on all stoppages, whether involving recognised trade union action or not,
would be included in the statistics. However, the regular series
does not distinguish between official and unofficial action.

Sympathetic action

Any sympathetic action taken by one group of workers in support of
another would be counted in the statistics, but in the absence of any
classification of cause of dispute it is not possible to distinguish such
action.

Political strikes

Political or protest stoppages, usually identified as having a wider
cause than most others, are measured and included in the statistics,
but are not distinguished separately.

Excluded sectors or groups

Generally there are no specific industrial sectors excluded from the statistics. However, the casual recording system used in Denmark tends to be biased in favour of the larger employers, these generally being the ones who respond to their employers' associations with information. In addition, the dependence on the employers' associations as the focus for information does mean that those employers without membership of such an association will be inhibited from supplying information. In the main, those affected will tend to be the smaller concerns, but because of the concentration of small employers in certain sectors (such as agriculture or retailing), the information base in these industries will be particularly weak.

In addition there are certain groups of workers prohibited from taking strike action. The police and the armed forces fall into this group but also there is a large number of employees in the public service (the *Tjenestemend*) who, in return for a privileged form of employment contract which provides for job security, forfeit the right to strike.

Measures and classifications

The main measures of activity used are:

number of stoppages;
number of workers involved;
number of working days lost.

The number of stoppages in some cases will include those involving more than one establishment, but with a common cause, or starting point and these are counted as one. The number of workers involved is calculated as the average number of workers taking part in the stoppage over its duration.

Industry

Stoppages are allocated to one of the eight broad groupings of the ISIC, with further subdivisions for manufacturing only into eight smaller groups.[1] The groups currently used are as follows: (1) agriculture; (2) manufacturing, further subdivided into (a) food and drink; (b) textiles, leather and clothing; (c) wood and furniture; (d) paper and graphics; (e) chemicals; (f) stone, clay and glass; (g) iron and metal; and (h) other manufacturing industries: (3) electricity, gas, heating and water; (4) construction; (5) commerce; (6) restaurants and hotels; (7) transport; and (8) other industries and services.

In the regular statistics, only those industries actually experiencing stoppage activity were listed up until 1977. Since that year the same eight groupings (with the eight subdivisions of manufacturing) have been published irrespective of no stoppage activity in some groups.

Cross-classifications

There are no cross-classifications of the statistics regularly produced. In fact the Danish statistics are the least detailed of all the nine countries examined in this study.

Availability of the information

The main source of information on stoppages during the year appears in the *Nyt Fra* (News From) series from Danmarks Statistik. The relevant one for stoppages (*Arbejdsstandsninger*) usually appears about mid-April, reporting on the statistics for the previous full year.

Other regular Danmarks Statistik publications carrying details of stoppages (but with the same range of information as the newsletter mentioned above) include the annual *Statistiske Efterretninger* and the less detailed *Statistik Arbog*.

Note

1. Up until 1976 the seventh group, transport, was divided into land and sea transport but this was discontinued with the 1977 figures.

Table 5.1 Denmark Summary statistics

	1972	1973	1974	1975	1976	1977	1978	1979	1980	1981
Number of stoppages	35	205	134	147	204	228	314	218	225	94
Number of workers involved	7,601	337,100	142,352	59,128	87,224	36,305	59,340	156,589	62,073	53,463
Number of working days lost	21,800	3,901,200	184,200	100,100	210,300	229,700	128,800	173,000	186,700	651,600

Source: Nyt Fra Danmarks Statistik, Arbejdsstandsninger, Danmarks Statistik.

Table 5.2 **Denmark** Working days lost by industry (000s)

	1972	1973	1974	1975	1976	1977	1978	1979	1980	1981
1. Agriculture	–	–	–	–	–	–	–	–	0.1	–
2. Manufacturing	21.0	2,473.9	177.2	94.0	190.3	202.1	65.9	101.5	154.2	516.0
(a) Food, drink	3.4	127.2	28.6	28.3	17.0	6.6	14.8	33.9	83.0	160.0
(b) Textiles, leather, clothing	1.3	217.3	6.1	0.9	2.1	0.9	3.2	1.6	4.1	1.5
(c) Wood, furniture	2.1	154.0	0.5	–	–	0.3	–	1.2	1.0	0.1
(d) Paper, graphics	2.4	299.0	9.6	10.0	10.7	128.9	2.7	3.7	26.5	344.4
(e) Chemicals	–	57.4	0.8	0.2	2.2	0.3	2.2	1.9	10.0	–
(f) Stone, clay, glass	5.0	230.7	7.4	1.0	75.7	–	–	–	–	–
(g) Iron, metal	6.8	1,388.3	124.2	53.6	82.6	58.7	41.8	50.4	26.8	8.8
(h) Other	–	–	–	–	–	6.4	1.2	8.8	2.8	1.2
3. Electricity, gas, heat, water	–	–	–	–	–	–	–	–	–	–
4. Construction	0.3	867.5	1.4	–	4.5	0.8	0.3	0.8	1.0	0.1
5. Commerce	0.4	41.1	1.6	1.2	8.1	2.6	1.6	5.4	5.7	1.1
6. Restaurants, hotels	–	–	–	–	–	1.1	42.1	–	–	–
7. Transport*	0.1	255.5	4.0	4.3	2.3	11.1	11.4	22.8	8.5	27.1
(a) Land	0.1	–	3.6	4.3	1.2	–	–	–	–	–
(b) Sea	–	–	0.4	–	1.1	–	–	–	–	–
8. Other (incl. services)	–	263.2	–	0.6	5.1	12.0	7.5	42.5	17.2	107.3
All industries and services	21.8	3,901.2	184.2	100.1	210.3	229.7	128.8	173.0	186.7	651.6

* From 1977 land and sea transport were not identified separately.
Source: Nyt Fra Danmarks Statistik, Arbejdsstandsninger, Danmarks Statistik.

6 FRANCE

Method of measurement

Information on stoppages of work is gathered on a continuous basis by the Statistical Division of the French Ministry of Labour, the Ministère du Travail. The Ministry receives this information from a range of established sources including direct reporting from the central offices of the nationalised industries and the monitoring of press reports. However, the main source of detail is at a local level where local labour inspectors (*inspecteurs de travail*), on hearing of a dispute, inform the appropriate Ministry of Labour office in the area (*département*). The labour inspectors are responsible for a wide range of issues such as health and safety matters, for example, and the notification of disputes is considered almost a by-product of their primary function.

Employers are under no legal obligation to inform either the Labour Inspectorate or the Ministry of Labour of the occurrence of a stoppage at their establishment, though once a stoppage has come to the attention of the authorities then the employer is supposed to freely provide the essential details of it. The details are gathered with the use of a standard form. One such form is completed by the employer at the start of the dispute and returned to the appropriate office (at the *département* level) and another is completed when the dispute has ended, thus providing the necessary details over its whole duration. In many cases the stoppage will be of short duration anyway, so the first form issued will then suffice for collecting the complete details of the dispute. The use of two forms only usually applies for those stoppages lasting in excess of 48 hours.

The French statistics differ from those of the other countries covered in this study in their specific treatment of those stoppages which have a wider cause and effect. Since 1975 the statistics have distinguished between what are called *conflits localisés* and *conflits généralisés*. *Conflits localisés* are those stoppages which have a clearly identifiable starting point and are relatively confined, usually to a single sector or company. If a stoppage starts off as, or becomes during its course, more diffuse in character, perhaps—covering a number of different industrial sectors and even possibly a number of regions, then the stoppage is categorised as a *conflit généralisé*.

The vast majority of stoppage activity is attributable to local disputes in one specific establishment and the statistics since 1975 verify this. Thus, over the period 1975–81, approximately 84.5 per cent of all working days lost recorded in the statistics were attributable to *conflits localisés* only.

Definitions
Conditions for inclusion
There is no minimum size condition imposed before a stoppage is included in the French statistics. Thus, all stoppages coming to the attention of the Ministry of Labour are included (however, see political strikes below).

Definition of establishment
The establishment is taken to be the reporting unit in most cases and this is usually the place at which the stoppage first occurs. In the case of those stoppages considered to fall into the category of *conflits généralisés*, it is more difficult to gather such specific information since in many such cases the outbreak of the stoppage will have happened simultaneously in a number of establishments, and so figures may be estimated from pieces of information gleaned from other sources such as press reports.

Lockouts
The incidence of lockouts in France is probably extremely rare. Employers have been reluctant to use such action because they are almost certain to be regarded as illegal except in special circumstances.[1] However, the stoppage statistics include any lockouts but do not distinguish them separately.

Indirect effects
Any indirect effects of industrial action at the same establishment are excluded from the statistics.

Secondary effects
The effects of a stoppage on establishments outside the striking establishment are not measured. This also applies to those categorised as *conflits généralisés*, where the principal criterion for inclusion will be active participation in the dispute.

Official/unofficial disputes

The degree of union recognition accorded a dispute or the level of union involvement has no effect on the inclusion of a stoppage in the statistics. Accordingly official and unofficial actions are not distinguished separately in the statistics.

Sympathetic action

Any sympathetic action taken by groups of workers outside the original striking establishment would be counted as new disputes and included in the statistics accordingly. Widespread sympathetic action could transform what started as a local dispute into a broader *conflit généralisé*. However, in the absence of a classification by cause of stoppage, the extent of sympathetic action is not known.

Political strikes

Any stoppages of a political protest nature would not be included in the statistics which are related solely to those issues connected with the terms and conditions of work. However, it may be the case that some of the widespread stoppages classified under *conflits généralisés* may have some underlying political or protest motive.

Excluded sectors or groups

The statistics do not measure those disputes in the agricultural sector or in public administration (*les administrations publiques*— civil servants at a local and national level), the reasons for which are unclear though historical precedent would seem to account for it. However, excluding these two sectors does eliminate a large proportion of the employed labour force from the measurement base, accounting for approaching four million or about 20 per cent of the total.

In addition to the two excluded sectors, certain groups of workers are forbidden to take strike action. These mainly consist of the police, armed forces and, more vaguely, anyone who in taking strike action puts the public at risk. Firemen or air traffic controllers (who decide to walk out in the middle of their shift) might be included in this category.

Measures and classifications

There are four main measures of activity regularly used in the statistics:

number of stoppages;
number of establishments affected;
number of workers involved;
number of working days lost.

The number of stoppages measures the individual issues which have emerged as a dispute, while the number of establishments shows the extent of the stoppage. Reference to Table 6.1 illustrates the significant differences between the two measures over the period 1972–81, with a consistently high number of establishments affected in relation to individual stoppages. However, these figures do include the *conflits généralisés* which by definition will have a widespread effect in terms of establishments involved.

The number of workers involved represents the average number on strike during the stoppage where this is calculable from the data supplied by the employer. Workers involved together with the duration of the stoppage are used to determine the number of working days lost by industry and region for *conflits généralisés*. Days are not allocated to each group or region but presented in total only.

Industry

The current industrial classification was introduced in 1976 and uses a basic thirty-four groupings. The older classification (*ancienne nomenclature*) used fewer groupings (twenty-seven in all) and this is not strictly comparable with the new one. Table 3.3 uses the older classification in order to provide comparable figures over the period 1972–81.

Region

The regularly published statistics each month carry details of working days lost by the following twenty-two regions: Île de France; Champagne-Ardenne; Picardie; Haute Normandie; Centre; Nord-Pas-de-Calais; Lorraine; Alsace; Franche-Comté; Basse Normandie; Pays de la Loire; Bretagne; Limousin; Auvergne; Poitou-Charentes; Aquitane; Midi-Pyrénées; Bourgogne; Rhône-Alpes; Languedoc-Rousillon; Provence-Alpes-Côte d'Azur; and Corse. The annual statistics provide more detail by each of the ninety-six administrative *départements*.

Currently only the classifications by industry and by region are published. Prior to 1970, the data was also broken down by cause, duration and type of settlement.

Cross-classifications

Apart from the main single classifications listed above, only two cross-classifications are published (annually):

working days lost per 100 employees X region and by industry (*conflits localisés* only);
establishments affected/workers involved/working days lost X nature of dispute (*conflits généralisés* only).

Availability of the information

The main source of information on the monthly statistics of stoppages is the *Bulletin Mensuel des Statistiques du Travail,* the main journal of the French Ministry of Labour. Aggregated annual information is published once a year by the Ministry, usually in a special issue of the above mentioned journal in the series *Supplément au Bulletin Mensuel des Statistiques du Travail.* This contains the most readily available detailed analysis of the statistics.

Note

1. See Kennedy, T., *European Labor Relations* (Lexington, D. C. Heath, 1980), Chapter 2.

Table 6.1 France Summary statistics

	1972	1973	1974	1975	1976	1977	1978	1979	1980	1981
For disputes resolved during year										
Number of stoppages	3,464	3,731	3,381	3,888	4,348	3,302	3,206	3,104	3,542	2,504
Number of establishments affected	72,882	35,995	14,771	23,946	35,534	20,287	12,178	22,010	4,829	3,875
Number of workers involved (000s)	2,721.3	2,246.0	1,563.5	1,827.1	2,022.5	1,919.9	704.8	967.2	500.8	329.0
For all disputes during year										
Number of working days lost (000s)	3,755.3	3,914.6	3,380.0	3,868.9	5,010.7	3,665.9	2,200.4	3,656.6	1,674.3	1,495.6

Source: Bulletin Mensuel des Statistiques du Travail, Ministère du Travail.

Table 6.2 France Working days lost by region (000s)

Region	1972	1973	1974	1975*	1976	1977	1978	1979	1980	1981
Île de France	305.8	625.5	729.7	902.6	623.1	317.0	446.5	403.0	170.1	245.5
Champagne-Ardennes	122.1	208.6	111.7	148.8	174.3	79.0	35.6	105.6	18.5	32.6
Picardie	82.8	129.1	90.4	152.5	233.6	53.8	51.9	129.9	33.5	19.7
Haute Normandie	80.1	80.1	129.1	103.5	121.1	65.7	82.9	71.4	67.4	48.7
Centre	84.8	132.2	52.5	102.6	162.8	75.0	39.1	65.4	33.9	26.9
Nord-Pas-de-Calais	219.3	253.3	342.3	226.8	405.4	199.7	202.7	259.1	147.9	137.0
Lorraine	100.1	110.3	122.0	144.4	153.0	56.1	107.4	174.5	96.6	79.1
Alsace	234.0	55.3	18.5	18.3	67.7	77.1	36.1	35.6	24.5	29.6
Franche-Comté	81.9	110.3	32.5	59.1	66.2	28.9	13.8	309.8	24.3	39.1
Basse-Normandie	52.3	65.5	86.0	37.4	85.7	36.8	112.1	143.5	30.3	28.7
Pays de la Loire	237.9	210.9	107.6	195.8	114.7	177.4	85.0	129.7	46.1	58.3
Bretagne	145.2	72.8	111.8	72.1	95.7	51.7	80.0	66.4	57.9	54.7
Limousin	60.1	40.7	14.9	26.0	17.8	15.2	8.1	59.3	12.5	15.8
Auvergne	93.6	105.2	71.5	94.4	79.2	175.1	23.4	81.4	41.5	35.8
Poitou-Charentes	67.2	76.6	44.5	57.8	190.0	24.9	16.5	32.1	23.7	24.5
Aquitaine	82.5	91.2	110.2	94.7	102.7	86.3	61.5	73.3	45.1	77.6
Midi-Pyrénées	81.3	90.9	80.3	49.1	57.7	70.0	36.6	60.0	30.0	90.0
Bourgogne	67.9	73.5	49.6	162.5	143.1	69.7	31.0	70.0	75.9	35.6
Rhône-Alpes	603.0	513.3	490.6	393.9	481.7	295.5	207.1	507.8	214.1	143.2
Languedoc-Roussillon	56.1	63.9	64.6	33.7	66.4	65.4	21.9	76.1	27.8	24.6
Provence-Alpes-Côte d'Azur	382.9	329.3	187.2	197.1	175.1	187.2	245.9	128.3	91.0	71.2
Corse	—	0.8	11.0	4.9	5.1	1.5	0.2	2.4	1.9	2.3
Stoppages affecting several regions	514.4	475.4	320.9	254.7	432.8	225.4	135.7	187.7	196.9	121.4
France	3,755.3	3,914.6	3,380.0	3,532.7	4,054.9	2,434.4	2,081.0	3,172.3	1,511.3	1,441.9

* From 1975 figures are for *conflits localisés* only.
Source: Bulletin Mensuel des Statistiques du Travail, Ministère du Travail.

Table 6.3 France Working days lost by industry (000s)

	1972	1973	1974	1975*	1976	1977	1978	1979	1980	1981
1. Water, gas, electricity	115.3	575.4	95.3	70.3	270.7	42.8	31.9	2.5	0.8	0.9
2. Oil and motor fuels	9.5	204.4	3.9	0.8	2.3	12.8	8.3	0.3	1.0	–
3. Solid fuels	26.6	128.6	2.6	–	10.1	2.1	–	–	–	–
4. Mining of metals and construction materials	157.8	70.5	8.4	21.5	35.4	1.8	–	13.0	1.8	3.7
5. Metal production	107.7	125.9	110.3							
6. Metal processing	174.3	235.3	296.7	1,573.9	1,296.9	795.8	775.4	1,295.9	465.6	439.0
7. General mechanics	203.3	107.6	130.3							
8. Motor vehicle manufacture	440.7	55.2	330.5							
9. Electricity manufacture	120.3	110.2	121.5	361.2	372.2	83.1	184.0	641.9	109.7	109.2
10. Glass, ceramics and construction materials	78.2	65.4	80.9	92.4	129.0	97.0	87.3	101.6	45.3	94.9
11. Building & public works	204.8	210.9	143.8	198.5	182.2	189.2	104.9	109.9	124.9	118.3
12. Chemical and rubber industry	180.5	72.8	91.3	154.0	222.8	273.1	50.7	146.6	156.8	37.0
13. Agriculture, food	77.9	38.7	57.2	86.4	147.5	104.5	42.7	73.0	62.8	54.0
14. Textiles	96.5	105.1	130.0	87.7	186.4	90.5	63.2	45.2	40.9	93.2

15. Clothing and material work	24.8	76.3	29.7	73.1	74.2	63.3	68.4	67.5	49.4	27.4
16. Leather and furs	24.0	91.2	72.2	24.4	19.1	33.4	7.5	19.1	10.0	43.2
17. Wood and furniture	36.2	90.7	48.4	65.8	50.6	69.1	18.3	32.9	20.7	19.7
18. Paper, packaging	48.2	73.6	24.8	46.1	211.5	40.5	38.3	26.2	24.8	37.6
19. Graphics	43.8	513.3	104.6	212.1	203.2	56.0	20.5	39.9	28.7	22.8
20. Other industries	32.2	64.2	54.5	95.4	107.4	20.7	43.7	60.4	58.6	40.8
21. Transport	435.7	329.5	306.7	198.1	232.1	250.1	131.2	213.4	196.7	131.8
22. Food and agricultural commerce	19.8	–	38.6 ⎫	89.4	143.2	97.6	66.0	113.2	55.6	73.5
23. Non-food commerce	41.4	–	58.8 ⎭							
24. Banks, insurance, agencies	110.3	0.7	754.7	40.8	47.5	38.4	17.1	131.3	13.9	49.1
25. Entertainment	1.2	–	–	–	–	–	–	–	–	–
26. Sanitation	7.8	569.1	4.0	16.7	26.7	9.8	4.0	11.7	10.5	11.1
27. Professional services	24.3	–	23.8	24.1	84.0	62.8	317.6	26.8	32.8	34.7
Stoppages involving several industries	912.2	–	256.5	–	–	–	–	–	–	–
All industries and services	3,755.3	3,914.6	3,380.0	3,352.7	4,054.9	2,434.4	2,081.0	3,172.3	1,511.3	1,441.9

*From 1975 figures are for *conflits localisés* only.

Source: *Bulletin Mensuel des Statistiques du Travail*, Ministère du Travail.

7 FEDERAL REPUBLIC OF GERMANY

Method of measurement

The main statistical series on strikes and lockouts is compiled by the national statistical office of the Federal Republic of Germany (FRG), the Statistisches Bundesamt, from the information received by each of the statistical offices of the eleven federal state governments or *Lander*. The data reaches the national statistical office only after the regional statistical series has been compiled.

All employers have a statutory obligation to inform the local office of the federal employment service, the Bundesanstalt für Arbeit, of the incidence of a dispute at their establishment. In response to this notification the employment office sends the employer a prescribed form on which to enter full details of the start of the strike or lockout. In most cases one form will suffice for gathering complete details of the stoppage, but in the few cases where the action is protracted, a second form is issued to cover the termination of the stoppage as well as the details since the first form was returned to the employment office. A combination of the legal obligation on employers to provide details of the stoppage and the vigilance of employment office staff mean that a high proportion of all disputes are reported.

The federal employment service, though acting as the principal agent for the collection of stoppage details, does not itself publish such data, leaving this task to the national statistical office. This arrangement goes back to 1949 when an internal agreement was reached between the two agencies by which the forms are turned over at a federal state level. This of course means that the production of the regular statistical series is carried out independently of any involvement the federal employment bureau might have in individual disputes, for example in discussing arrangements for mediation.

Definitions
Conditions for inclusion

Those stoppages lasting less than one working day or involving less than ten workers are excluded from the statistics, except where the aggregate of working days lost exceeds 100. This minimum size was based on and is currently the same as the UK minimum, and was adopted in the Federal Republic after the end of the 1939–45 war.

Definition of establishment

The recording unit is the establishment at which the dispute first breaks out. Those disputes which have a common cause or starting point but affect several establishments simultaneously would be recorded as separate stoppages, one for each establishment.

Lockouts

Lockouts are included in the statistics and are measured separately. A strike and a lockout occurring simultaneously at the same establishment would be counted separately and appear in the appropriate series, though such cases are rare in practice and would be subjected to the necessary caveats in the published tables. For example in 1979, the last year in which recorded lockouts occurred, aggregation of working days lost through strikes and lockouts gives a total of 649,603. However, due to the simultaneous occurrence of a number of strikes and lockouts at the same establishments resulting in the double-counting of 166,520 days, the true working days lost figure is actually 483,083. Out of a total number of strikes plus lockouts of forty-eight in that year, eight involved a strike and a lockout at the same time. Hence in Germany the main measure of number of stoppages is proxied by the number of establishments involved. More statistical details are given in Table 7.1.

Indirect effects

Any indirect effects on workers at the same establishment as that experiencing the stoppage are not measured.

Secondary effects

Any effects of the stoppage at establishments other than where the dispute first occurred are not measured.

Official/unofficial disputes

All action, whether involving a trade union or not, is included provided that it satisfies the other criteria for inclusion, but the different types of action are not identified separately in the statistics.

Sympathetic action

Any sympathetic action taken by workers (or management in the form of a lockout), whether at the striking establishment or not would be included as a separate dispute, but because there is no analysis of the statistics by cause or major issue, such action could not be identified separately. However, as Kennedy points out, in any case under German labour law such action would be illegal.[1]

Political strikes

As with sympathetic stoppages, political strikes would be considered illegal in the Federal Republic and so do not represent a major factor in the statistics. However, if (illegal) political stoppages do occur they would be included in the statistics.

Excluded sectors or groups

All sectors of industry are included in the regular statistics if stoppages occur in them. However, certain government employees (known as the *Beamte*) are prohibited from taking strike action in return for a privileged form of employment contract, the major provision of which is to give recipients security of tenure in their posts. Generally the *Beamte* include such groups as the police, armed forces and senior officials of federal and national governments. In addition, the prohibition on taking strike action extends to certain public service employees in key services such as the air traffic controllers, for example.

This in effect means that a large segment of the labour force will not be involved in strike action under normal circumstances. Though it is difficult to be precise about actual numbers involved, it will be an important factor to take into account when comparing Germany's strike record with those of other countries.

Measures and classifications

The main measures of activity used are:

    number of establishments involved;
    number of workers involved;
    number of working days lost.

The number of establishments involved records separately any strikes and lockouts occurring simultaneously at the same establishment. The measure, however, can be taken to be a good proxy for the number of stoppages recorded. Table 7.1 shows the separate statistics for strikes and lockouts as well as the net aggregate of the two.

The number of workers involved is taken to be the average number over the duration of the stoppage unless more precise information is available which permits actual workers involved to be recorded, usually for stoppages of relatively short duration.

Industry

Stoppages are allocated according to the broader industrial groupings of the Standard Germany Industrial Classification. This consists of nine broad groups as follows: (1) agriculture, forestry, fishing: (2) energy, water, mining; (3) manufacturing; (4) building; (5) commerce; (6) transport and communications; (7) banking and insurance; (8) services; and (9) local government and social security. These nine are further disaggregated into smaller industry groupings. In the regular analysis of the stoppage statistics by industry, only those sectors experiencing stoppages during the period are listed, as in, for example, *Streiks und Aussperrungen* (see 'Availability of the information' below).

Regions

All analyses of the data use the eleven *Landern* or federal regions of: Schleswig-Holstein; Hamburg; Niedersachsen; Bremen; Nordrhein-Westfalen; Hessen; Rheinland-Pfalz; Baden-Württemburg; Bayern; Saarland; and West Berlin.

Duration

Only three categories of duration are used in the regular statistics: under seven days; seven to twenty-four days; and more than twenty-four days, all according to the length of time the stoppage lasts for. Details are only published for the measure number of workers involved.

Cross-classifications

The following cross-classifications of the data are regularly produced:

workers involved/working days lost X region (strikes and lockouts together);

establishments involved/workers involved/working days lost X broad industry group X region (strikes and lockouts separately);

workers involved X duration X region (strikes and lockouts separately).

Availability of the information

As already mentioned, the main publications carrying the statistics of stoppages of work emanate from the Statistisches Bundesamt. The first release of the information is via an annual press communication which usually appears about February each year and provides only broad details of the previous full year's stoppages.

The main publication for the statistics is the annual report *Bevölkerung und Erwerbstätigkeit, Reihe 4.3, Streiks und Aussperrungen* which is published about March. This includes the most comprehensive breakdown of the statistics as well as commentary on the trend of stoppages over the year. Comprehensive details also appear in the annual publication *Arbeits und Sozialstatistik* though much later than the alternative sources of information.

Note

1. Kennedy, T., *European Labour Relations* (Lexington, D. C. Heath, 1980), p. 180.

Table 7.1 Germany Summary statistics

	1972	1973	1974	1975	1976	1977	1978	1979	1980	1981
Strikes										
Number of establishments involved	54	732	890	201	950	81	618	32	132	297
Number of workers involved	22,908	185,010	250,352	35,814	117,450	34,437	298,774	62,517	45,159	253,334
Number of working days lost	66,045	563,051	1,051,290	68,680	411,683	23,681	2,547,810	405,156	128,386	58,398
Lockouts										
Number of establishments involved	—	—	1	—	559	2	657	16	—	—
Number of workers involved	—	—	22	—	58,359	329	274,094	40,903	—	—
Number of working days lost	—	—	110	—	136,167	1,226	2,813,956	244,447	—	—
Strikes and lockouts*										
Number of establishments involved	54	732	889	201	1,481	79	1,239	40	132	297
Number of workers involved	22,908	185,010	250,352	35,814	169,312	34,437	487,050	77,326	45,159	253,334
Number of working days lost	66,045	563,051	1,051,290	66,680	533,696	23,681	4,281,284	483,083	128,386	58,398

*Figures are net and count those stoppages involving a strike and a lockout simultaneously as one.
Source: *Bevölkerung und Erwerbstätigkeit: Reihe 4.3*, Statistisches Bundesamt.

Table 7.2 Germany Working days lost by region

Region	1972	1973	1974	1975	1976	1977	1978	1979	1980	1981
Schleswig-Holstein	400	1,151	17,481	3,439	41,679	–	6,488	–	1,028	2,206
Hamburg	9,217	–	24,600	1,335	19,383	–	49,089	–	9,424	1,697
Niedersachsen	10,561	13,288	53,414	–	42,946	–	3,693	363	7,814	8,066
Bremen	1,830	30,663	524,578	387	9,064	6,059	31,720	28,504	7,814	544
Nordrhein Westfalen	43,110	134,430	187,631	13,236	99,894	2,511	936,394	369,555	20,899	12,278
Hessen	–	9,584	45,997	3,822	59,526	256	28,044	5,929	11,478	1,435
Rheinland-Pfalz	64	684	9,500	143	13,389	315	482	44	3,639	3,140
Baden-Württemburg	783	346,756	55,186	16,846	40,643	4,450	1,397,850	–	27,864	29,032
Bayern	80	2,007	42,576	29,472	60,924	9,466	18,099	761	31,118	–
Saarland	–	24,488	5,058	–	5,380	624	1,839	–	180	–
Berlin (West)	–	–	85,269	–	18,855	–	74,172	–	10,011	–
Germany	66,045	563,051	1,051,290	68,680	411,683	23,681	2,547,870	405,156	128,386	58,398

Note: Table includes days lost through strikes only.
Source: *Bevölkerung und Erwerbstätigkeit: Reihe 4.3*, Statistisches Bundesamt.

Table 7.3 **Germany** Working days lost by industry

	1972	1973	1974	1975	1976	1977	1978	1979	1980	1981
1. Agriculture, forestry, fishing	–	–	–	–	–	–	–	–	–	–
2. Energy, water supply, mining	–	18,443	36,219	–	–	–	–	–	–	–
3. Manufacturing (excluding building)	64,067	544,379	574,687	39,101	390,409	23,138	2,394,035	404,395	27,405	54,857
4. Building	–	–	–	29,472	–	210	73,221	–	–	–
5. Commerce	–	–	–	–	–	–	222	–	–	–
6. Transport and communications	1,978	–	217,173	–	–	333	78,618	761	100,981	450
7. Banking and insurance	–	–	886	–	–	–	–	–	–	–
8. Services	–	–	9,539	–	21,274	–	1,774	–	–	3,091
9. Local government and social security	–	229	212,786	107	–	–	–	–	–	–
All industries and services	66,045	563,051	1,051,290	68,680	411,683	23,681	2,547,870	405,156	128,386	58,398

Note: Table includes days lost through strikes only.
Source: *Bevölkerung und Erwerbstätigkeit: Reihe 4.3*, Statistisches Bundesamt.

8   IRELAND

Method of measurement

Collecting information on stoppages of work in Ireland is primarily the responsibility of the Department of Labour. The Department has traditionally collected such information in order to inform the government ministers of the progress in individual disputes, but the use of the information is now much wider. The Department passes on the information it has on individual disputes to the Central Statistics Office (CSO), which has responsibility for publishing the regular details.

The gathering of information on individual disputes is a continuous process and principally depends on the local employment offices. On hearing of a dispute in their area of operation, the local office sends out a prescribed form to the employer (this has already been referred to on page 44) who is requested to fill out full details of the stoppage and return copies of the form to the Department of Labour and the CSO.[1] The provision of such information by the employer is voluntary, as is the reporting of a dispute to the Department of Labour in the first instance. The occurrence of stoppages is also gleaned from press reports, trade unions and other diverse sources and then followed up in the usual way.

The CSO not only publishes the data but also collects its own information on stoppages. Such information comes mainly from the local offices of the Department of Social Welfare, since managers have instructions to report any stoppages that come to their notice, usually through those on strike claiming assistance. Local managers are not, however, under any obligation to declare such information and in most cases the incidence of such reporting will tend to fluctuate with the workload at each office.

Definitions

Conditions for inclusion

A minimum size is applied to all stoppages before their inclusion in the statistics. Those stoppages lasting less than one working day or where fewer than ten man days are lost in total are excluded from the statistics.

Definitions of establishment

The local unit at which the dispute first occurs is taken to be the reference point for the statistics, though a stoppage simultaneously involving a number of different establishments would be counted only as one stoppage. However, the number of establishments involved are measured separately and so can be identified (see 'Measures and classifications' below).

Lockouts

Lockouts are thought to be non-existent in Ireland, but if they did occur they would be measured and included but not identified separately in the statistics.

Indirect effects

In most cases any indirect effects at the establishment where the stoppage began would be included. Such effects are not generally identified separately in the regular statistics, though the quarterly stencilled sheet issued by the CSO (see 'Availability of the information' below) does separate out the number of workers indirectly involved for each individual dispute. However, such information is not presented in an aggregated annual form.

Secondary effects

No attempt is made to measure any secondary effects of a stoppage, therefore such effects will be excluded from the statistics.

Official/unofficial disputes

The degree of trade union involvement in a dispute is not strictly shown in the regular statistics, though some idea of this involvement can be gauged from the classification by cause of dispute. One of the categories covers stoppages caused by 'trade union questions or refusal to conclude a collective agreement', though this mainly relates to specific union issues as opposed to the level of official action.

Sympathetic action

Any action taken in support of workers already on strike is measured and included in the regular statistics. Furthermore, it can be identified separately in the classification by cause of dispute.

Political strikes

Strikes with a political basis are considered to be extremely rare in Ireland, but if they did occur then they would be included in the statistics though not distinguished separately.

Excluded sectors or groups

There are no specific industrial sectors excluded from the statistics and the only occupations specifically prohibited from taking strike action are the police and the armed forces.

Measures and classifications

The main measures of activity regularly used are as follows:

number of stoppages;
number of establishments involved;
number of workers involved;
number of working days lost.

As already mentioned, under 'number of stoppages' those stoppages which affect a number of different establishments are counted as one, the establishments also being shown separately. The number of workers involved represents the average number taking action during the course of the stoppage.

Cause

There is a relatively detailed classification of stoppages under their main cause. The first classification group covers those concerned with collective bargaining issues and is divided into: (a) concerning trade union questions or refusal to conclude a collective agreement; and (b) concerning conditions of employment in relation to the following issues: (i) wages; (ii) hours of labour; (iii) engagement or dismissal of workers, redundancy, etc.; (iv) holidays with pay; (v) re-organisation, demarcation, transfers, etc.; and (vi) other matters. The second main classification group concerns those issues not related to collective bargaining and here two sub-classifications are used: (a) sympathetic disputes; and (b) other matters.

   In addition to the classifications listed above and which appear in the main publication carrying details of stoppages, the quarterly *stencilled sheet* already referred to lists the more specific cause of each individual stoppage recorded.[2]

Industry

The groupings by industry used in the regular statistics are based on the Standard Irish Classification with seventeen broad groups of: (1) agriculture, forestry and fishing; (2) mining, quarrying and turf production; (3) food; (4) drink and tobacco; (5) textiles; (6) clothing and footwear; (7) woodworking and furniture; (8) paper and printing; (9) chemicals and chemical products; (10) clay products, glass, cement, etc.; (11) metals and engineering; (12) other manufacturing; (13) construction and repair work (including building); (14) electricity, gas, water and sanitary services; (15) commerce; (16) transport, storage and communications; and (17) services.

Duration

The duration of stoppages is classified into eight bands measured in days as follows: 1–2 days; 3–5 days; 6–10 days; 11–20 days; 21–30 days; 31–50 days; 51–100 days; and over 100 days. This classification is published for all three main measures of activity, the exception being establishments involved.

Importance of dispute

The relative size of stoppages are identified in two classifications. The first involves classifying the number of disputes by the number of establishments involved (one, two, three, four and more than four). The second classification is by number of workers involved: less than 10; 10–20; 21–30; 31–50; 51–100; 101–200; and over 200 workers. Both classifications show the number of stoppages only.

Cross-classifications

There are no cross-classifications of the data regularly produced. However, the quarterly stencilled sheet from CSO provides more details of each individual stoppage recorded, including the town location of the affected establishment, its name and the trade union involved (if appropriate), plus the so-called 'classes of workers' involved, which can give an idea of broad occupational groups affected.

Availability of the information

The first source of information on stoppages is a quarterly stencilled sheet emanating from the CSO (and available on a request basis only). This contains individual details of each stoppage recorded over the quarter (ending in March, June, September and December).

The main details are aggregated once a year and feature as an article usually in the December issue of the *Irish Statistical Bulletin* from the CSO.[3]

Notes

1. Additional copies are usually sent to the Department of Social Welfare (one each for the Unemployment Benefit Decisions Section and the Disability Benefit Section) and to the Registrar of the Labour Court.
2. These causes are much more specific and serve to underline the difficulties to be encountered in grouping the multifarious causes into a limited number of broad issues. For example, causes are listed such as 'unauthorised absence', 'allocation of trainee driver' or 'dismissal of shop steward' alongside the other specific details of the dispute, including the name of the employer affected.
3. The actual issue carrying details of disputes over the previous year has varied. Recently it has been the December issue, but in 1980 it was the September one and before that year it tended to be the March issue.

Table 8.1 Ireland Summary statistics

	1972	1973	1974	1975	1976	1977	1978	1979	1980	1981
Number of stoppages beginning in year	131	182	219	151	134	175	152	140	130	117
Establishments involved	232	265	248	183	231	222	199	186	158	126
Workers involved	22,274	31,761	43,459	29,124	42,281	33,805	32,558	49,621	30,879	31,958
Working days lost	206,955	206,725	551,833	295,716	776,949	442,145	624,266	1,464,952	412,118	433,979

Source: Irish Statistical Bulletin, Central Statistics Office.

Table 8.2 Ireland Working days lost by industry

	1972	1973	1974	1975	1976	1977	1978	1979	1980	1981
1. Agriculture, forestry, fishing	640	27	2,100	–	–	1,100	–	–	–	3,380
2. Mining, quarrying and turf production	1,355	21,343	11,895	11,237	46,632	10,900	142,618	6,478	6,699	106,580
3. Food	9,018	17,720	15,367	32,866	37,350	40,254	10,066	19,008	44,977	39,893
4. Drink and tobacco	252	1,676	49,838	35,359	–	6,430	1,294	4,081	7,365	28,910
5. Textiles	30,335	3,886	9,883	31,115	9,238	37,191	6,211	3,413	26,121	9,008
6. Clothing and footwear	5,772	7,677	7,471	4,515	7,324	5,475	342	374	17	450
7. Woodworking and furniture	1,300	295	4,741	457	357	3,910	–	1,558	600	5,512
8. Paper and printing	913	10,024	1,791	1,445	27,979	81	3,580	1,743	10,268	3,190
9. Chemicals and chemical products	47,146	2,504	10,611	2,817	11,844	8,489	35,941	15,347	7,371	39,224
10. Clay products, glass, cement, etc.	9,843	490	17,834	6,842	14,053	12,407	27,043	3,445	19,250	3,965
11. Metals and engineering	43,948	21,314	43,726	75,104	24,929	137,344	66,833	97,021	16,078	47,257
12. Other manufacturing	15,454	5,435	10,953	13,373	3,506	12,649	64,821	12,625	770	–
13. Construction and repair work (incl. building)	22,494	12,963	8,082	52,614	33,853	47,070	26,304	18,426	68,192	32,459
14. Electricity, gas, water and sanitary services	700	8,508	2,926	3,395	1,800	1,110	401	4,078	16,965	9,450
15. Commerce	4,497	44,080	33,681	14,619	482,213	42,851	52,600	60,167	55,142	55,002
16. Transport, storage, communications	11,796	36,843	247,222	5,213	59,653	28,482	174,378	1,205,664	46,493	40,238
17. Services	1,492	11,940	73,712	4,745	16,218	46,402	11,834	11,524	85,810	9,461
All industries and services	206,955	206,725	551,833	295,716	776,949	442,145	624,266	1,464,952	412,118	433,979

Source: Irish Statistical Bulletin, Central Statistics Office.

Table 8.3 Ireland Working days lost by cause

	1972	1973	1974	1975	1976	1977	1978	1979	1980	1981
1. Related to collective bargaining										
(a) Concerning trade union questions or refusal to conclude a collective agreement	3,114	6,641	11,840	3,161	–	30,155	1,974	3,338	9,082	26,963
(b) Concerning conditions of employment in relation to:										
(i) wages	97,345	73,990	147,544	135,758	610,496	204,914	410,808	1,407,030	248,914	212,364
(ii) Hours of work	1,296	3,840	218,674	10,806	300	–	1,220	4,668	305	16,081
(iii) Engagement, dismissal, redundancy, etc.	48,249	33,340	55,046	116,066	120,139	134,524	80,935	25,326	77,354	87,673
(iv) Holidays with pay	163	2,331	–	–	–	–	–	–	3,056	–
(v) Reorganisation, demarcation, transfer, etc.	28,203	12,328	29,348	4,100	5,499	23,486	86,929	375	7,439	28,280
(vi) Other matters	27,909	68,504	88,878	25,521	38,125	42,035	35,394	16,081	65,968	61,318
2. Not related to collective bargaining										
(a) Sympathetic disputes	276	1,345	184	218	1,216	1,375	75	–	–	1,300
(b) Other matters	400	4,406	319	86	1,174	5,656	6,931	8,134	–	–
All causes	206,955	206,725	551,833	295,716	776,949	442,145	624,266	1,464,952	412,118	433,979

Source: Irish Statistical Bulletin, Central Statistics Office.

9 ITALY

Method of measurement

The focus for the recording of stoppages of work in Italy is the local police. When a strike or lockout occurs, the employer is obliged by law to inform the local police office of the basic facts. However, the law surrounding the provision of such information is vague and in fact there does not seem to be an explicit law making it obligatory for employers to inform the police of a stoppage of work. Rather the obligation is implicit in a general law which requires such information relating to potential acts of public disobedience to be divulged to the police. Thus the involvement of the police in the collection of information on stoppages dates from the time when a strike was regarded as a potential act of civil disorder. The system of measurement has remained, however, even though the right to take strike action has become enshrined in Italian labour law (see Chapter 16).

The police only act as a focus for finding out about the outbreak of a stoppage of work. The police inform the local offices of the Ministry of Labour and Social Security (the Ministero del Lavoro e della Previdenza Sociale) who themselves are responsible for gathering details of the stoppage direct from the employer. The Ministry of Labour passes the full details gathered to the Italian central statistical office, the Istituto Centrale di Statistica (ISTAT), which has the responsibility of compiling and publishing the regular statistics.

Definitions

Conditions for inclusion

There is no minimum size for inclusion in the regular statistics. All those stoppages coming to the notice of ISTAT are included. Nevertheless, it is inevitable that some of the stoppages of very short duration will escape the notice of the measurement system.

Definition of establishment

Given the emphasis in the information system on the local police as the focus for initial contact, the establishment is taken to be the local unit at which the stoppage first takes place. Depending on the nature of subsequent action in different establishments, in most cases they will be counted as separate disputes.

Lockouts

Lockouts are included in the regular statistics but are not distinguished separately. However, they are not thought to be common in practice.

Indirect effects

Any indirect effects of a strike or lockout at the same establishment are included but are not distinguished separately in the statistics.

Secondary effects

Any secondary effects at establishments other than those involved with the stoppage directly are not measured.

Official/unofficial disputes

The regular statistics include both official union-sanctioned disputes and disputes without full union recognition, though in the statistics they are not distinguished.

Sympathetic action

Action taken by one group of workers in sympathy with a group already on strike would be included in the statistics and would be counted as a separate stoppage. The analysis by cause identifies such action separately under the title 'solidarity' (see Table 9.4).

Political strikes

The measurement of strike action taken with the primary motive of a political protest were not measured at all up to 1974. However, from 1975 a special classification of cause of dispute, 'stoppages by other causes', was introduced to cover such action instigated by causes other than those directly connected with the terms and conditions of work. This category covers not only politically motivated strikes, but also takes in any stoppage which cannot be reasonably placed in the main category. In practice the special classification contains almost exclusively those strikes of a political nature, given the relatively high number of large-scale protest strikes throughout Italy.

In terms of working days lost attributable to this special cause, the five years after its introduction show that it accounted for 19 per cent of all working days lost during the period 1975–9. This has implications for the value of the series of statistics covering the period either side of the introduction of this new classification. Prior to 1975 any action of a political nature was excluded from the statistics and so the annual information up to and including 1974 will be deficient by probably up to one fifth, though this proportion will tend to vary from year to year (see Table 9.4).

Excluded sectors or groups

There are no specific sectors of industry excluded from the statistics and the only occupational group prohibited from taking strike action is the military.

Measures and classifications

There are three main measures of activity used in the regular statistics:

number of stoppages;
number of workers involved;
number of working hours lost.

The Italian statistics are unique in using the number of working *hours* lost as opposed to working *days* lost, the case in all the other countries covered in this study. Though the use of hours does permit a more precise measure of the effects of a stoppage on working time, it can cause problems when trying to compare the data with those of other countries. The problem is that using a standard divisor of eight to arrive at working days lost assumes, wrongly, that the average working day in Italy is constant at eight hours. Apart from annual changes which have brought the average normal hours worked now down to about thirty-five hours per week, the length of the working day is very much dependent on such factors as occupation, sex, overtime or the incidence of shift working. As a result, the application of an eight-hour day can only be at best a convenient method of arriving at some notion of working days lost, comparable with the statistics of other countries.

Cause

Since 1975 there are two broad categories used to describe the main cause of a stoppage; (1) those stoppages connected with the terms and conditions of work; and (2) stoppages by other cause (but mainly those of a political nature, see page 106). Prior to 1975 only those stoppages falling into category (1) were measured.

Stoppages connected with the terms and conditions of work are further divided into the following five sub-groups; (a) renewal of contract; (b) salary or economic vindication; (c) dismissal, suspension of workers or reductions in hours; (d) solidarity; and (e) other causes.

Industry

In most analyses of the regular statistics, twenty groupings are used, derived from the Standard Italian Classification of Industrial Activity. Within these twenty groups there are ten major sectors as follows: (1) agriculture, forestry and fishing; (2) mining and extractive; (3) manufacturing; (4) construction; (5) electricity, gas and water; (6) commerce; (7) transport and communications; (8) banking and insurance; (9) social services and activities; and (10) public administration. A further ten groups are sub-divisions of manufacturing industry.

Region

Details of all main measures are published for the twenty Italian regions of: Piemonte; Valle d'Aosta; Lombardia; Trentino-Alto Adige (sometimes further divided into Bolzano-Bozen and Trento); Veneto; Friuli-Venezia Giulia; Liguria; Emilia-Romagna; Toscana; Umbria; Marche; Lazio; Abruzzi; Molise; Campania; Puglia; Basilicata; Calabria; Sicilia. and Sardegna.

Size of stoppage

There are two measures used of the relative size of a stoppage. The first uses the number of workers involved with sixteen bands ranging from zero to ten workers, up to 50,001 and over. The second measure uses fifteen bands of working hours lost from the smallest of 500 and under, to the largest of 2,000,001 and over.

Cross-classifications

The following cross-classifications are regularly published in addition to the single classifications of the three main measures of activity listed above:

Stoppages/workers involved/working hours lost
X cause X industry;
X cause X region;
X industry X region.

Availability of the information

The first release of the statistics is via a monthly newsheet from ISTAT, titled *Lavoro e Retribuzioni.* However, the main sources are the monthly ISTAT publication, *Bollettino Mensile di Statistica*, and the more comprehensive annual volume on labour statistics, the *Annuario di Statistiche del Lavoro*. The latter volume, though containing the most comprehensive collection of stoppage statistics, is not generally published until around eighteen months after the relevant year covered by the statistics.

Table 9.1 **Italy** Summary statistics

	1972	1973	1974	1975*	1976	1977	1978	1979	1980	1981
Number of stoppages	4,765	3,769	5,174	3,601	2,706 (2,265)	3,308 (2,748)	2,479 (2,062)	2,000 (1,655)	2,238 (1,895)	2,204
Number of workers involved (000s)	4,405	6,133	7,824	14,109	11,898 (10,814)	13,803 (11,472)	8,774 (7,330)	16,238 (14,402)	13,825 (13,490)	8,227
Number of working days lost† (000s)	17,060	20,492	17,033	23,791 (22,673)	22,205 (20,124)	14,495 (11,551)	8,905 (7,330)	24,089 (21,919)	14,400 (13,915)	9,211

*Figures in brackets from 1975 onwards are comparable figures to the years 1970–4 (i.e. political stoppages excluded). Figures for 1981 are not yet available.

†Figures for working days lost are the total of working hours lost divided by eight.
Source: *Annuario di Statistiche del Lavoro*, Istituto Centrale di Statistica.

Table 9.2 Italy Working days lost by region* (000s)

Region	1972	1973	1974	1975†	1976	1977	1978	1979	1980
Piemonte	1,815	3,070	2,559	2,135	2,286	1,796	599	3,244	2,772
Valle d'Aosta	29	51	35	58	34	48	26	62	22
Lombardia	3,975	5,655	3,530	4,335	5,281	2,949	1,544	5,194	3,039
Trentino-Alto Adige	177	289	227	283	279	149	75	301	117
Veneto	1,208	1,563	1,384	1,457	1,518	984	853	1,631	804
Friuli-Venezia Giulia	515	800	484	597	611	545	452	1,009	515
Liguria	691	709	503	689	487	330	131	752	309
Emilia-Romagna	2,364	2,445	2,451	3,334	3,398	2,114	1,649	3,721	2,005
Toscana	1,467	1,648	1,612	2,780	2,669	1,484	1,154	2,735	1,652
Umbria	129	115	98	206	186	108	41	178	137
Marche	180	269	284	453	385	291	208	424	269
Lazio	904	667	552	1,086	1,037	666	445	1,381	428
Abruzzi	210	200	191	277	150	138	109	215	174
Molise	28	23	23	45	27	23	20	43	67
Campania	917	923	722	1,047	771	589	357	740	385
Puglia	714	764	703	2,248	1,591	996	418	1,033	734
Basilicata	88	81	61	125	78	77	53	51	28
Calabria	213	97	109	298	234	129	156	166	126
Sicilia	1,002	804	1,056	1,604	703	763	380	848	470
Sardegna	434	318	452	732	483	319	236	361	350
Italy	17,060	20,492	17,033	23,791	22,205	14,495	8,905	24,089	14,400

† Political strikes are included from 1975 onwards.
Source: Annuario di Statistiche del Lavoro, Istituto Centrale di Statistica.
*Figures for working days lost are the total of working hours lost divided by eight. Due to rounding, the sum of the constituent items may not agree with the totals.

Table 9.3 Italy Working days lost by industry* (000s)

	1972	1973	1974	1975†	1976	1977	1978	1979	1980†
1. Agriculture, forestry, fishing	1,239	743	1,214	3,188	2,006	1,132	346	1,252	947
2. Mining & extractive	225	180	95	192	96	58	39	71	55
3. Manufacturing:	8,925	14,372	10,189	8,328	12,196	8,451	4,328	13,728	9,226
Food, drink, tobacco	313	129	616	291	349	524	138	291	477
Textiles	344	1,705	949	874	1,373	846	742	1,400	711
Clothing	192	207	417	402	399	254	143	202	194
Footwear, leather & connected	47	224	210	203	195	101	69	81	87
Wood & furniture	58	284	208	249	286	107	82	203	165
Metallurgical, mechanical	5,647	9,840	5,665	3,977	7,189	4,477	1,905	9,160	5,702
Mineral	443	498	248	220	350	263	185	416	278
Chemical	1,652	995	1,241	1,350	1,428	1,161	849	1,541	1,253
Paper and poly-graphics	156	360	251	304	249	399	144	333	187
Others	74	130	385	460	378	321	70	99	172
4. Construction	1,885	283	1,243	1,941	1,701	1,172	923	1,898	884
5. Electricity, gas, water	118	253	171	149	94	46	66	54	84
6. Commerce	142	1,058	726	1,081	1,396	191	332	804	429
7. Transport & communications	938	1,606	775	1,569	1,014	627	497	1,136	398
8. Banking & insurance	908	48	181	221	623	61	171	887	202
9. Social services & activities	1,423	682	915	1,259	962	1,199	1,653	1,272	736
10. Public administration	1,258	1,267	1,527	5,864	2,119	1,560	550	2,988	1,440
All industries and services	17,060	20,492	17,033	23,791	22,205	14,495	8,905	24,089	14,400

† Political strikes are included from 1975 onwards.
* Note: Figures for working days lost are the total of working hours lost divided by eight. Due to rounding the sum of the constituents may not agree with the totals.
Source: Annuario di Statistiche del Lavoro, Istituto Centrale di Statistica.

Table 9.4 Italy Working days lost by cause* (000s)

	1972	1973	1974	1975	1976	1977	1978	1979	1980
1. Stoppages connected with conditions/terms of work	17,060	20,492	17,033	22,673	16,464	9,846	6,129	20,614	9,402
(a) Renewal of contract	10,116	14,467	3,690	2,706	11,181	3,107	2,002	15,999	2,743
(b) Salary/economic vindication	3,501	3,039	10,522	9,741	1,626	3,066	1,664	1,990	1,557
(c) Dismissal, suspension of workers, reduction in hours	579	206	182	532	451	600	705	406	1,849
(d) Solidarity	582	1,265	485	51	1,122	128	170	49	2,768
(e) Other	2,281	1,515	2,155	9,643	2,084	2,945	1,588	2,170	485
2. Stoppages by other causes†	–	–	–	1,118	5,742	4,650	2,776	3,475	4,998
All causes	17,060	20,492	17,033	23,791	22,205	14,495	8,905	24,089	14,400

* Note: Figures for working days lost are the total of working hours lost divided by eight. Due to rounding, the sum of the constituent parts may not agree with the totals.

† This category began in 1975 and examines stoppages instigated by causes other than conditions of work, e.g. political strikes, requests for social reform, national and international events, etc.

Source: *Annuario di Statistiche del Lavoro*, Istituto Centrale di Statistica.

Method of measurement

In the Netherlands the collection of information on stoppages of work is a continuous process involving the constant monitoring of local labour markets by the appropriate employment offices in the area (there are approximately 130 such local offices spread throughout the country). This local focus inevitably means that the quality and coverage of the information depends to a great extent on the available time and vigilance of local employment office staff.

When the local office becomes aware of a stoppage of work in its area (this could be from diverse sources such as a press report or from verbal information, for example), further details are sought directly from the employer (according to the information required) on the prescribed form used for the purpose but, in fact, completed by the local employment office. It is usual to allow about one week to pass before full details of the stoppage are sought to allow the dispute to run its course, since most tend to start and finish in a relatively short period of time. In those cases where a dispute lasts longer than the week or so that is allowed to elapse, initial details are sought and are then followed up by a further enquiry when the dispute has ended. Clearly the method outlined for recording the details could mean that some of the information relies on the memory of the employer which may be somewhat vague relating to a strike that possibly happened a week ago. Also, any information given by the employer is given voluntarily and this can lead in some cases to incomplete records of some particular disputes.

The problems with the quality of the data on stoppages is recognised by the body responsible for co-ordinating and publishing the regular statistical series, the Dutch national statistical office, the Centraal Bureau voor de Statistiek (CBS). In particular, there is concern about the non-recording of many stoppages, especially those of very short duration, which usually escape the notice of the local employment office staff. In an effort to alleviate some of this downward bias in the statistics, therefore, the CBS has revised the original series covering 1970–80 in the light of reports in the press on stoppages that were not included in the original series.[1] As an indication of the degree of revision required in the original statistics, taking the ten-year period 1971–80 the original figures recorded a total number of stoppages of 288. The revised figures from the CBS increased this figure to 351 based on the retrospective look at newspaper reports. This means that at least 18 per cent of stoppages were not recorded.

In terms of working days lost the difference is not so pronounced, with 31,397 days lost going unrecorded representing approximately 2 per cent of the revised total. From this it would seem that the usual methods of measurement are picking up a high proportion of the time lost through disputes and those not being recorded are mainly the smaller stoppages which may be high in number, but have only a small effect on the aggregate working days lost.

Table 10.1 Netherlands Stoppages in 1971–80, original and revised figures compared

	Original figures 1971–80	Revised figures 1971–80	Difference
Number of stoppages	288	351	+63.0
Average number of workers involved (000s)	222.5	273.5	+51.0
Number of working days lost (000s)	1,437.2	1,468.6	+31.4

Source: Sociale Maandstatistiek, CBS.

Table 10.1 illustrates the discrepancy for all three major measures of activity over the ten-year period 1971–80. It should be noted that the figures used in Tables 10.2 to 10.4 inclusive use the original figures throughout, primarily to achieve compatibility with the 1981 data which is not yet available in an adjusted form.

Definitions

Conditions for inclusion

There is no minimum size applied to a stoppage before its inclusion in the statistics, though as outlined above the very small disputes involving relatively few lost working days will tend to be missed out altogether.

Definition of establishment

The establishment, as used for recording purposes, is taken to be the place at which the stoppage first occurred. Thus a dispute with a common cause but involving two different establishments would be counted as two separate disputes.

Lockouts

The occurrence of lockouts is considered to be small in number in the Netherlands, though in the absence of separate statistics on them it is difficult to be precise about this. Nevertheless, lockouts are included in the regular statistics when they occur.

Indirect effects

Any indirect effects of a stoppage on workers at the same establishments are included where possible, but are not identified separately in the statistics.

Secondary effects

No account of secondary effects of any stoppage are taken in the regular statistics. However, there is some attempt to measure its extent where this is possible, but the data collected is not made widely available.

Official/unofficial disputes

For all disputes the extent of any trade union involvement is assessed and shown separately together with the major reason for the stoppage. However, the detail is limited to whether a union was involved or not. The proportion of total stoppages with some degree of union involvement is generally not that much higher than those without. For example, 53 per cent of all recorded stoppages in 1979 (before subsequent adjustments) had some union involvement. However, when working days lost are taken into account the effect of union involvement is much more pronounced. Taking the 1979 figures again, 89 per cent of total days lost due to stoppages in that year were in those with some degree of union involvement.

Sympathetic action

Any action taken in sympathy by workers in either the same establishment or in a different establishment to where the original action took place would be measured and counted as a separate stoppage. However, such action is not separately identified in the statistics.

Political strikes

Any strike action with a political motive would be included and would constitute a so-called 'protest' stoppage as identified separately in one of the categories of cause of stoppage (see below). However the category of cause would include all protest stoppages, only some of which will be of a political nature.

Excluded sectors or groups

There are no particular sectors of industry precluded from the statistics though certain groups of workers are prohibited from taking strike action. The restriction mainly applies to the police and armed forces with the addition of certain groups of public service employees such as local government officials and teachers, for example.

Measures and classifications

The main measures of activity used are:

number of stoppages;
number of workers involved;
number of working days lost.

The number of workers involved is presented in two forms: either the average number of workers involved during the course of the stoppage or the highest number. The former measure, however, is the one most commonly used for the analyses of the statistics and, as has already been indicated in Part I, is the measure most consistent with the practice in other countries.

Cause

The broad categories of cause regularly used in an effort to describe what is called 'the point of issue' are: (1) pay questions: (a) increases in wages; (b) other wage matters; (2) working conditions; and (3) protest strikes. These categories of cause are shown separately for those stoppages involving trade unions and those without any such involvement.

Industry

The Standard Dutch Industrial Classification is used and in the annual series of statistics only those industry groups recording any strike action are listed. The groups are relatively broad and consist of: (1) food, drink and tobacco; (2) textiles and clothing;

(3) wood and furniture; (4) paper; (5) graphics and publishing; (6) chemical and petroleum; (7) artificial and synthetic fibres; (8) rubber and synthetics processing; (9) building materials, earthenware and glass; (10) metal; (11) transportation equipment; (12) building and installations; (13) commerce, catering and repairing; (14) transport, storage and communications; (15) banks, insurance, agents, etc.; (16) social, cultural and other institutions; and (17) other industries.

Regions

The regular statistics are produced for the eleven provinces of the Netherlands: Groningen; Friesland; Drenthe; Overijssel; Gelderland; Utrecht; Noord-Holland; Zuid-Holland; Zeeland; Noord-Brabant; and Limburg.

Duration

Five broad bands of duration are used, measured in the number of working days the stoppage lasts for. The bands are: less than one; 1 to less than 2; 2 to less than 5; 5 to less than 10; and 10 days and over.

Method of settlement

The way in which strikes are terminated are categorised into three methods: (1) direct negotiations between employer and employees; (2) negotiations with trade unions; and (3) other ways of settlement.

Cross-classifications

Apart from the straightforward single classifications of the three main measures by cause, industry, region, duration and method of settlement, only one cross-classification is regularly published:

stoppages/average number of workers involved/working days lost
X cause X involvement of trade union (i.e. involved or not).

Availability of the information

The first release of any information on either a particular stoppage or a latest series of statistics may be via a bulletin in the series *Statistisch Bulletin*, though the practice is irregular.

The main publication carrying annual details of stoppage activity is the CBS publication *Sociale Maandstatistiek*. The series appears in the May issue and covers the previous full year. More detailed information, particularly relating to local statistics on stoppages, may be available on a request basis from the CBS, though such additional information will be limited as most of the usable data is published.

Note

1. The revised series first appeared in the CBS publication *Sociale Maandstatistiek* (June 1982).

Table 10.2 Netherlands Summary statistics

	1972	1973	1974	1975	1976	1977	1978	1979	1980	1981
Number of stoppages	31	153	14	5	11	9	9	30	11	11
Average number of workers involved	19,548	58,113	2,979	268	15,255	35,945	2,548	31,844	20,412	8,600
Number of working days lost	134,187	583,783	6,854	480	13,984	236,090	2,834	306,730	55,442	24,114

Source: Sociale Maandstatistiek, Centraal Bureau voor de Statistiek.

Table 10.3 Netherlands Working days lost by province

Province	1972	1973	1974	1975	1976	1977	1978	1979	1980	1981
Groningen	1,127	8,653	560	–	–	7,447	–	170	44	–
Friesland	53	3,798	–	–	–	3,843	–	–	–	400
Drenthe	4,594	18,443	80	–	4	11,791	342	878	–	40
Overijssel	–	37,207	462	–	–	13,136	–	677	440	–
Gelderland	–	82,414	2,400	80	–	14,253	39	442	1,616	50
Utrecht	40	58,983	1,202	–	–	4,887	–	–	–	–
Noord-Holland	35,501	84,869	60	–	8,740	24,585	922	5,800	10,079	988
Zuid-Holland	87,608	176,015	–	35	5,180	115,985	1,261	295,366	13,138	21,180
Zeeland	–	35,510	–	175	–	15,309	–	137	22,881	656
Noord-Brabant	5,264	68,955	2,090	135	60	20,612	270	2,118	1,679	800
Limburg	–	8,936	–	55	–	4,242	–	1,142	4,565	–
Netherlands	134,187	583,783	6,854	480	13,984	236,090	2,834	306,730	54,442	24,114

Source: Sociale Maandstatistiek, Centraal Bureau voor de Statistiek.

Table 10.4 Netherlands Working days lost by industry

	1972	1973	1974	1975	1976	1977	1978	1979	1980	1981
1. Food, drink & tobacco	117	5,400	–	80	–	19,451	386	4,611	2,510	40
2. Textiles & clothing	51	88,499	–	–	–	1,543	–	172	–	–
3. Wood & furniture	3	1,198	–	–	–	–	–	–	–	–
4. Paper	756	96	80	–	12	255	–	635	2,400	–
5. Graphics & publishing	–	560	–	–	20	10,452	–	–	200	–
6. Chemical & petroleum	–	–	–	–	–	24,120	546	25,372	6,203	–
7. Artificial & synthetic fibres	5,264	–	–	–	–	–	–	–	–	–
8. Rubber & synthetics processing	–	–	22	–	–	–	–	–	–	–
9. Building materials, earthenware & glass	–	5,995	5,128	175	4	652	265	14	–	–
10. Metal	5,203	209,937	–	–	205	22,893	–	566	1,312	706
11. Transport equipment	112,040	271,813	–	–	214	21,291	–	3,038	39,380	–
12. Building & installations	–	63	29	–	–	52,581	–	–	281	–
13. Commerce, catering & repairing	–	–	–	–	–	1,234	–	35	–	1,200
14. Transport, storage & communications	10,753	222	1,595	225	13,514	81,594	984	272,272	1,948	19,500
15. Banks, insurance agents	–	–	–	–	15	–	–	–	–	1,730
16. Social, cultural & other institutions	–	–	–	–	–	24	163	15	208	938
17. Other industries	–	–	–	–	–	–	490	–	–	–
All industries and services	134,187	583,783	6,854	480	13,984	236,090	2,834	306,730	54,442	24,114

Source: Sociale Maandstatistiek, Centraal Bureau voor de Statistiek.

Table 10.5 Netherlands Working days lost by cause

	1972	1973	1974	1975	1976	1977	1978	1979
1. Pay questions	11,168	582,597	3,823	–	13,734	234,637	1,934	294,539
(a) Rise in wages	10,650	3,181	2,650	–	13,734	233,548	–	294,201
(b) Other wage matters	518	579,416	1,173	–	–	1,089	1,934	338
2. Working conditions	9,858	1,039	950	270	185	1,416	900	6,262
3. Protest strikes	113,161	147	2,081	210	65	37	–	5,929
All causes	134,187	583,783	6,854	480	13,984	236,090	2,834	306,730

Source: Sociale Maandstatistiek, Centraal Bureau voor de Statistiek.

11 UNITED KINGDOM

Method of measurement

Responsibility for both the collection and publication of information on industrial disputes rests with the Department of Employment (DE). The information flows in on a continuous basis with the main source being the local Unemployment Benefit Offices (UBOs) of which there are over 1,000 throughout the UK. The UBO managers get their information from a variety of sources, in addition to the obvious route through their own knowledge of what is going on in their particular area of operation. Press reports, for example, are sometimes the first indication that a dispute has broken out; sometimes trade unions might intimate such information directly to the UBO.

The local UBO managers can seek further details of a stoppage directly from the employer, though the employer is not obliged to provide the information requested, but gradually a fuller picture of the stoppage is built up. In some cases this will not be necessary, however, since some of the nationalised industries, for example, provide details of stoppages affecting them directly to either the UBO or DE.

Though the system is fairly informal in its method of operation, it does have the advantage of being well established. In terms of its coverage of all disputes that occur, an assessment of the success of the system really depends on which of the main measures is used. There have been a small number of studies which shed some light on the accuracy of the DE figures. Most recently Brown has reported that only about 17 per cent of all stoppages occurring (of any size) were covered by the DE figures (though this increases to 40 per cent for those lasting one day or more),[1] but in terms of working days lost the percentage covered by the DE figures is much higher at approximately 94 per cent. Clearly then it is the smaller stoppages which are at the same time the most prolific, but also the most likely ones to be missed by the measurement system, though this has little effect on the working days total since most days lost are due to a small number of large stoppages over a given period.

Definitions

Conditions for inclusion

All those stoppages involving less than ten workers or lasting less than one working day are not counted, except where the aggregate of working days lost exceeds 100. There are particular difficulties in ensuring that all relevant stoppages are included in the statistics, especially those near the margins of this minimum size definitions, but this (as outlined above) is reckoned to affect the number of stoppages measure more than the other two.

Definitions of establishment

The local unit or establishment is taken to be the recording unit for the statistics, though there are problems when one dispute affects a number of separate establishments. In such cases those which can be identified as having a common cause and starting point would be counted as only one stoppage.

Lockouts

The incidence of a lockout would be recorded on the same basis as for strikes, though they are not distinguished separately in the statistics. However, the incidence of lockouts in the UK is reckoned to be small in practice.

Indirect effects

Any indirect effects of a stoppage on workers at the same establishment are measured where it is possible. Indirect action is shown separately in some of the analyses of the data (see Table 11.2).

Secondary effects

Any secondary effects of a stoppage at other establishments are not recorded by the statistics.

Official/unofficial disputes

Both official and unofficial disputes are recorded and included in the statistics and are shown separately in a limited number of analyses of the data. Table 11.1 shows the relative proportion of official to unofficial action over the period 1971–80 for all three main measures of activity. The average figures show broadly that by far the majority of stoppages are classed as unofficial (95.3 per cent), though they accounted for comparatively smaller proportions of total workers involved (57.6 per cent) and a much smaller proportion of total working days lost (29.0 per cent).

Table 11.1 UK Proportion of official and unofficial action (percentages)

Year	Stoppages* Official	Stoppages* Unofficial	Workers involved* Official	Workers involved* Unofficial	Working days lost Official	Working days lost Unofficial
1971	7.2	92.8	32.1	67.9	74.2	25.8
1972	6.4	93.6	36.9	63.1	76.2	23.8
1973	4.6	95.4	26.2	73.8	27.9	72.1
1974	4.3	95.7	28.8	71.2	47.7	52.3
1975	6.1	92.9	10.1	89.9	19.1	80.9
1976	3.4	96.6	6.9	93.1	14.4	85.6
1977	2.9	97.1	17.7	82.3	24.8	75.2
1978	3.6	96.4	12.3	87.7	43.1	56.9
1979	3.9	96.1	79.6	20.4	79.8	20.2
1980	5.0	95.0	48.7	51.3	84.3	15.7
Average 1971-80	4.7	95.3	42.4	57.6	61.0	29.0

* For stoppages beginning in year only.
Source: Employment Gazette, Department of Employment.

Sympathetic action

Any action taken in sympathy with other workers already on strike is measured and identifiable separately in the classification by cause of dispute. Table 11.5 shows that the incidence of sympathetic action is relatively small, accounting for only 0.3 per cent of the total working days lost due to all stoppages over the ten-year period 1972–81.

Political strikes

The official statistics only cover those stoppages concerned with the terms and conditions of work and by definition any strikes of a political nature (where they are identifiable as such) would be excluded. However, though such strikes would not be included in the statistics, they may be recorded by the DE in the normal process of information gathering.

Excluded sectors or groups

There are no exclusions of industrial sectors from the statistics, and the only groups prohibited from taking strike action are the police and the armed forces.

Measures and classifications

The following main measures of activity are used regularly in the published statistics:

number of stoppages;
number of workers involved;
number of working days lost.

The measure 'number of stoppages' where possible records individual stoppages only, some of which may affect a number of different establishments simultaneously. The measure 'workers involved' is based on the maximum number of workers taking part or indirectly affected during the course of stoppage.

Cause

The classification by cause is taken to be that cause disclosed by the parties involved and may, therefore, mask the true or underlying cause of the dispute. Since 1973 the following seven broad categories have been used (1) pay, subdivided into: (a) wage rates and earnings levels, and (b) extra wage and fringe benefits; (2) duration and pattern of hours worked; (3) redundancy questions; (4) trade union matters; (5) working conditions and supervision; (6) manning and work allocation; and (7) dismissal and other disciplinary measures.[2] Also, up to 1974 there was an additional category covering miscellaneous causes but this was discontinued from 1975 onwards. A separate category also lists the amount of action attributable to sympathetic support.

Industry

The regular analyses of the data either use the twenty-seven groupings of the UK Standard Industrial Classifications (SIC) as listed in Table 11.4, or a more detailed derivative using fifty MLH headings within the SIC orders.

Region

Analyses of the stoppages data are only given by the eleven standard planning regions of the UK as follows: South East; East Anglia; South West; West Midlands; East Midlands; Yorkshire and Humberside; North West; North; Wales; Scotland; and Northern Ireland. More detailed information may be available on a request basis from the DE.[3]

Duration

The duration of stoppages is broken down into eleven divisions measured in working days, from 'not more than one day', to the highests category of 'over 50 days'. Aggregations of these duration periods may also appear in the published statistics.

Principal disputes

For those disputes involving more than 5,000 working days lost, comprehensive details are provided including industry group, towns where the dispute occurred, as well as some details of occupations involved. This classification of principal disputes represents the only detail provided on the broad occupational groups affected.

Importance of stoppage

The relative size of stoppages is analysed by seven bands of working days lost from the smallest of 'under 250 days', to the largest of '50,000 days and over'. A further classification aggregates stoppages according to the number of workers involved, with ten bands from 'under 25 workers' up to '10,000 workers and over'.

Cross-classifications

In addition to the single classifications listed above, the following cross-classifications of the data are regularly published:

Stoppages/workers involved/working days lost X industry X cause
Workers involved/working days lost X industry X location X occupation X cause
Workers involved/working days lost X industry X regions.

Availability of the information

The main statistics of stoppages of work are published first in the official journal of the DE, *Employment Gazette*. There is a monthly series of the latest available information which provides the basis for the annual aggregation of the statistics appearing in a provisional form usually in the January issue (and covering the previous full year), followed by the finalised version in either the June or July issue.

A number of other publications draw on the *Employment Gazette* statistics to report annotated tables, such as those in the *Monthly Digest of Statistics* or the *Annual Abstract of Statistics* for example. More details can be found in Walsh *et al.*[4]

Notes

1. Brown, W. (ed.), *The Changing Contours of British Industrial Relations* (Oxford, Basil Blackwell, 1981).
2. The categories used prior to 1973 were as follows:

1. Wage disputes of which:
   (a) claims for increases
   (b) other wage disputes
2. Hours of work
3. Demarcation disputes
4. Disputes concerning employment or discharge of workers (including redundancy questions)
5. Other disputes mainly concerning personnel questions
6. Other working arrangements, rules and disciplines
7. Trade union status
8. Sympathetic action.

The changes were discussed more fully in the *DE Gazette* (February 1973), pp. 117-20.
3. For some more detailed regional analyses of strike data see Smith, C. T. B., Clifton, R., Makeham, P., Creigh, S. W. and Burn, R. V., *Strikes in Britain* (London, DE Manpower Paper No. 15, HMSO, 1978). This covers the period 1966-73.
4. Walsh, K., Izatt, A. and Pearson, R., *The UK Labour Market* (London, Kogan Page, 1980), Chapter 19.

Table 11.2 UK Summary statistics

	1972	1973	1974	1975	1976	1977	1978	1979	1980	1981
Number of stoppages (in progress)	2,530	2,902	2,946	2,332	2,034	2,737	2,498	2,125	1,348	1,344
(a) Beginning in year	2,497	2,873	2,922	2,282	2,016	2,703	2,471	2,080	1,330	1,338
(b) Carried over from previous year	33	29	24	50	18	34	27	45	18	6
Number of workers involved (000s)	1,734	1,528	1,626	809	668	1,166	1,042	4,608	834	1,513
(a) Stoppages beginning in year	1,722	1,513	1,622	789	666	1,155	1,001	4,584	830	1,499
– directly involved	1,448	1,103	1,161	570	444	785	725	4,121	702	1,326
– indirectly involved	274	410	461	219	222	370	276	463	128	173
(b) Stoppages carried over from previous year	12	15	4	20	2	11	41	24	4	14
– directly involved	5	13	3	10	2	7	36	22	3	10
– indirectly involved	7	2	1	10	–	4	5	2	1	4
Working days lost (000s)	23,909	7,197	14,750	6,012	3,284	10,142	9,405	29,474	11,964	4,266
(a) Stoppages beginning year	23,816	7,089	14,694	5,861	3,230	9,864	8,890	28,974	11,887	4,188
(b) Stoppages carried over from previous year	93	108	56	151	54	278	515	500	77	78

Source: Employment Gazette, Department of Employment.

Table 11.3 UK Working days lost by region† (000s)

Region	1972	1973	1974	1975	1976	1977	1978	1979	1980	1981
South East	1,671	1,207	1,339	964	511	1,839	2,683	4,487	439	843
East Anglia	190	202	73	40	20	159	115	548	58	80
South West	450	196	184	195	87	298	182	2,423	117	171
West Midlands	2,410	1,322	2,018	1,095	718	2,141	1,299	4,199	838	613
East Midlands	2,548	257	1,446	208	161	533	270	2,351	725	116
Yorkshire and Humberside	3,787	626	2,090	489	214	792	799	3,115	2,832	449
North West	3,475	1,326	1,736	765	549	1,934	1,983	4,516	533	692
North	2,869	850	1,849	1,004	267	698	481	2,164	2,006	341
Wales	2,123	337	1,325	255	299	667	444	1,642	2,918	292
Scotland	4,080	797	2,423	753	413	935	886	3,298	1,447	599
Northern Ireland	306	76	267	245	45	146	264	730	49	69
UK	23,909	7,197	14,750	6,012	3,284	10,142	9,405	29,474	11,964	4,266

†Due to rounding, constituent items may not agree with the totals.
Source: *Employment Gazette*, Department of Employment.

Table 11.4 UK Working days lost by industry* (000s)

	1972	1973	1974	1975	1976	1977	1978	1979	1980	1981
1. Agriculture, forestry and fishing	1	1	22	1	—	1	—	—	6	—
2. Mining and quarrying	10,800	90	5,628	56	78	97	201	128	166	237
3. Food, drink and tobacco	248	116	577	159	96	811	694	805	148	178
4. Coal and petroleum products	19	15	68	47	2	8	8	45	—	†
5. Chemical and allied industries	53	71	88	202	23	277	128	148	203	142
6. Metal manufacture	657	516	892	355	325	684	360	960	8,749	58
7. Mechanical engineering	1,375	809	627	732	301	890	698	7,345	479	214
8. Instrument engineering	107	29	131	21	19	83	8	505	10	13
9. Electrical engineering	1,307	516	1,246	984	223	943	487	5,491	97	205
10. Shipbuilding and marine engineering	796	268	693	509	62	163	160	303	195	230
11. Vehicles	2,086	2,444	2,033	1,122	895	3,094	4,046	4,835	491	956
12. Metal goods n.e.s	308	218	214	209	153	275	225	950	137	55
13. Textiles	236	140	236	257	39	209	130	71	35	21
14. Leather, leather goods and fur §	—	—	—	—	—	—	—	—	—	—
15. Clothing and footwear	38	53	19	93	27	56	47	38	7	18
16. Bricks, pottery, glass and cement	123	96	108	48	25	141	131	112	25	72
17. Timber, furniture, etc.	25	67	24	21	11	23	20	23	19	25
18. Paper, printing and publishing	87	80	275	105	40	175	301	715	281	51
19. Other manufacturing	411	265	267	136	69	225	234	203	19	55
20. Construction	4,188	176	252	247	570	297	416	834	281	86
21. Gas, electricity, water	17	313	57	10	52	83	65	38	19	20
22. Transport and communication	876	332	706	422	133	301	361	1,419	252	359
23. Distributive trades	7	20	114	66	14	95	63	75	34	74
24. Insurance, banking, etc.	1	†	4	2	4	5	1	6	14	13
25. Professional and scientific services	102	336	234	30	26	47	23	1,418	179	89
26. Miscellaneous services	14	25	41	50	36	26	80	641	36	20
27. Public administration	27	202	194	128	63	1,133	518	2,363	79	1,076
All industries and services	23,909	7,197	14,750	6,012	3,284	10,142	9,405	29,474	11,964	4,266

*Due to rounding, constituent items may not agree with the totals.
† Less than 500 working days lost.
§ Included in other categories.
Source: *Employment Gazette*, Department of Employment.

Table 11.5 UK Working days lost by cause* (000s)

	1973	1974	1975	1976	1977	1978	1979	1980	1981
1. PAY	5,147	13,109	4,448	1,831	8,223	7,414	27,139	10,611	2,630
of which:									
(a) Wage rates and earning levels	4,962	12,626	4,402	1,663	7,631	7,257	26,933	10,462	2,586
(b) Extra wage and fringe benefits	185	483	46	168	592	157	206	149	44
2. Duration and pattern of hours worked	55	201	25	40	26	238	94	103	210
3. Redundancy questions	144	99	211	199	166	108	181	321	618
4. Trade union matters	569	500	474	379	313	288	437	232	302
5. Working conditions and supervision	192	116	115	205	211	249	117	176	58
6. Manning and work allocation	441	409	400	399	905	765	684	225	182
7. Dismissal and other disciplinary matters	591	411	242	456	534	329	400	297	242
8. Miscellaneous†	7	–	–	–	–	–	–	–	–
All causes	7,146	14,845	5,914	3,509	10,378	9,391	29,051	11,965	4,244
Sympathetic action included in above	37	19	40	17	21	32	132	14	5

*Through stoppages beginning in the year only, but includes days lost in succeeding year as a result of stoppages continuing into that year. Due to rounding, constituent items may not agree with the totals.
†The miscellaneous causes category was discontinued from 1974.
Source: Employment Gazette, Department of Employment.

Method of measurement

Statistics on labour disputes have been collected in the USA since 1880 with a developing series of methodology used over this long period.[1] The main agency involved at present with the collection of information is the Bureau of Labor Statistics (BLS) a specialist part of the US Department of Labor (DoL). The BLS has been involved with the series since 1914 and the present statistics can find their origin in a series started in 1927.[2]

Most statistical series evolve and change through time and the strike statistics are no exception to this rule. However, the latest change to the statistics came about at the end of 1981, the end of the period of statistical coverage in this study, when the current series was restricted from its coverage of those stoppages involving six or more workers and lasting at least a shift or a full day, to those only involving 1,000 or more workers. The drastic rationalisation was mainly due to the implementation of budget reductions in the government statistical services. This means that the series prior to the change is effectively broken at the end of 1981 and the new, more restricted series begins in January 1982. The BLS have been able to derive a similar series covering the larger disputes of 1,000 or more workers to provide some continuity, but of course it will not be possible to have details of the smaller disputes under the new threshold for the post 1981 period.

The method of recording the disputes remains the same, however, and involves firstly the detection by the BLS of the occurrence of a strike or lockout and secondly the procurement of the necessary details of the dispute. The first stage of this process involves a continuing trawl of a variety of sources of information in an attempt to cover the maximum number of stoppages. The main sources of information used are as follows:

reports from daily and weekly newspapers throughout the country mainly provided by a commercial press clipping service;

information received from the Federal Mediation and Conciliation Service;

information compiled by the local offices of the state employment security agencies;

other state agencies such as the state mediation boards, and
   labor departments;
some individual employers and employers' associations; and
   trade unions, both directly and through their publications.

In addition, various other federal agencies and departments may
contribute information as and when available. The machinery of
information collection, though fragmented, is well established
and is thought to provide details of all major stoppages occurring,
with particularly good coverage of the two measures workers involved and working days lost.

The second stage of the information collection process involves
the gathering of the more precise details of the dispute. This is
done by sending out two questionnaires to the appropriate location
of the dispute, one to be filled in by the relevant management
representative and one by the trade union or employee representative. A period of three weeks is normally allowed for receipt of
at least one completed questionnaire, after which a non-response
is followed up with a second questionnaire and, failing that, tele-
grams or telephone may be used to secure the necessary details.

Neither the employer nor the striking employee or trade union
are compelled to give the requested information and in practice it
appears that the response rate is high from management but very
low from, in particular, the trade unions. The questionnaires seek
a lot of detailed information which may be more geared to those
with the time and secretarial back-up to fill them in, and this in
part may explain the reluctance of some trade union representatives
to complete their questionnaires. However, it does mean that the
details presented in the regular strike statistics tend to be largely
dependent on management information which may have a particular bias on such details as the cause of the stoppage.

Where two questionnaires are received and the details given do
not match, it may then be a case of the BLS attempting to again
establish actual details directly from the striking establishment,
so perhaps the fact that only one questionnaire is usually received
avoids what could potentially be a time-consuming job for the
BLS staff.

In most instances, the one questionnaire will be adequate to
cover the whole duration of the dispute since most are of short
duration. In those cases where a strike does continue for a long
period, then details will be sought initially by the questionnaire,
to be followed up during and at the termination of the strike by
subsequent requests for information.

The information collected from the returned questionnaires is coded for computer analysis and figures are issued in a provisional form every month. In some cases estimates based on past experience have to be made of the number of workers involved or working days lost to ensure the quick release of the monthly statistics, but these are updated when the full details become available.

Definitions

Conditions for inclusion

Until the end of 1981 all those strikes or lockouts which lasted for at least one full day or full shift and involved at least six or more workers were counted. From January 1982 only those stoppages involving 1,000 or more workers are counted, irrespective of the duration of the stoppage. Only data on the strikes above the minimum size are recorded and so no information is available in an unpublished form other than that described above.

Definition of establishment

The establishment is taken to be the plant or site at which the dispute first occurs. Where a strike covers more than one plant of the same company (in different locations) and with the same cause, it is counted as one stoppage. In the case of analyses of the data by state or sub-state breakdowns, individual plants would be ascribed the appropriate number of workers involved and working days lost according to the location of the plants.

Lockouts

Lockouts are included in the statistics but are not identified separately. Their use by US management is thought to be low in comparison to strikes by employees.

Indirect effects

Workers laid off as a result of a strike at the same establishment are counted where this is possible.

Secondary effects

The measurement system does not attempt to assess the level of secondary effects from the recorded stoppages.

Official/unofficial disputes

Both official and unofficial disputes as well as legal and illegal disputes are measured, the former being distinguished separately in the statistics to some extent by showing the degree of union involvement.

Sympathetic action

Workers taking sympathetic strike action at either the original striking establishment or at a completely different site, would be counted and can be identified separately under a sub-category of one of the major classifications of cause of dispute, namely 'inter-union or intra-union matters'.

Political strikes

Only those strikes directly concerned with the terms and conditions of employment are recorded; therefore, strikes of a political nature would not be included. However, it is conceivable that the political motives behind a strike may be concealed by an ostensible cause related to employment conditions.

Excluded sectors or groups

Some government employees have no-strike clauses in their contracts of employment. Federal employees, including police and the armed services, are not allowed to strike and some state government workers also have such a prohibition, though the groups covered vary from state to state. Despite the presence of certain restrictions, however, strikes still do occur, though most of the action taken by government employees is at a local level. In 1980 for example, out of a total number of working days lost during the year from strikes by government workers of 2,347,800, 95.4 per cent of them were attributable to local government, while only 4.2 per cent was accounted for by state government employees and 0.4 per cent by federal employees.[3]

The statistics exclude specifically the strikes of any US seamen in foreign ports or conversely, foreign seamen in US ports, but otherwise all types of worker would be included.

Measures and classifications

The main measures of activity regularly used are:

   number of stoppages;

number of workers involved;
number of working days lost (or idle).

The number of workers involved in a strike is taken to be the highest number of workers idle on any one day during the course of the strike, including those indirectly affected, at the striking establishment.

Cause

There is a comprehensive classification of the major issues involved with each dispute. The present classification has been in use since 1961 and uses the ten broad groupings of: general wage claims; supplementary benefits; wage adjustments; hours of work; other contractual matters; union organisation and security; job security; plant administration; other working conditions; and inter-union or intra-union matters. In addition, these major groupings are further subdivided into approximately fifty-five specific causes.

Industry

All strikes are classified by industry group using the comprehensive US Standard Industrial Classification Manual. In the few cases where a strike affects more than one industry, for the smaller stoppage it would be placed in that industry group where it first started; for larger stoppages each industry affected would be recorded as having a stoppage and the number of workers involved and mandays lost would be distributed accordingly.

The usual industrial classification contains twenty-nine industry groups with subdivisions into manufacturing and non-manufacturing industry (in effect primary industry and services). However, the annual BLS publication *Analysis of Work Stoppages* provides a very detailed breakdown of all three main measures of strike activity under the twenty-nine major groups.

Occupations

Since 1971 for government workers and since 1972 for all workers, the strike statistics have been classified by broad occupational groups. For all strikes (that is in both public and private sectors), seven broad groups are used as follows: professional and technical; clerical; sales; production and maintenance; protective; service; combinations. For government employees only a more detailed analysis is available listing individual occupations such as teachers, nurses, etc.

Regions

Information is grouped under the fifty states and the District of Columbia. Further analyses appear for the main metropolitan areas within the states and the District of Columbia, but they only cover the three main measures without further classification.

States are also grouped into ten standard federal regions and these have provided the basis for the regional analysis in Table 12.2. Constituent states for each of the regions are as follows:

Region I:	Connecticut Maine Massachusetts New Hampshire Rhode Island Vermont	Region II:	New Jersey New York
Region III:	Delaware District of Columbia Maryland Pennsylvania Virginia West Virginia	Region IV:	Alabama Florida Georgia Kentucky Mississipppi North Carolina South Carolina Tennessee
Region V:	Illinois Indiana Michigan Minnesota Ohio Wisconsin	Region VI:	Arkansas Louisiana New Mexico Oklahoma Texas
Region VII:	Iowa Kansas Missouri Nebraska	Region VIII:	Colorado Montana North Dakota South Dakota Utah Wyoming

Region IX:	Arizona	Region X:	Alaska
	California		Idaho
	Hawaii		Oregon
	Nevada		Washington

Duration

The following eight bands of duration are regularly used: one day; 2–3 days; 4–6 days; 7–14 days; 15–29 days; 30–59 days; 60–89 days; 90 days and over.

Principal disputes

A list of the principal disputes (usually those involving 1,000 or more workers) is compiled monthly listing the company involved and occupations, etc., affected by the dispute. More details are provided in the annual analysis on the stoppages involving 10,000 or more workers. Much of the information gathered for the stoppage statistics is subject to rules of confidentiality and details of individual stoppages are released only with the permission of the parties involved. However, since such details, especially for the larger strikes, are usually widely reported in the press anyway (where the BLS might have first learned of the dispute), requesting permission is usually a formality.

Method of settlement

The methods by which stoppages are settled are given for those where information is available. The broad categories are as follows: formal settlement reached, all issues resolved or procedure established for handling unresolved issues (shown separately in some analyses); no formal settlement because the action was a protest or sympathy strike of short duration; strike broken; work resumed under court injunction; and employer went out of business. A separate category lists those disputes where no information on settlement was provided but the proportion of total strikes without such information is usually quite small. For example, in 1980 only 9.1 per cent fell into this category.

Size of stoppage

Stoppages are classified according to the number of workers involved. Eight bands of size are used as follows: 6 and under 20 workers; 20 and under 100; 100 and under 250; 250 and under 500; 500 and under 1,000; 1,000 and under 5,000; 5,000 and under 10,000; and 10,000 and over. This latter category of 10,000 workers or more is also used for segregating the largest strikes for more detailed individual analysis.

Contractual status

The contractual position of the workers involved at the start of the strike is given using four broad categories of: negotiation of first agreement; renegotiation of agreement (expiration or re-opening); during term of agreement (negotiation of new agreement not involved); and no contract or other contract status. The vast majority of all stoppages occurring during a typical year involves the renegotiation of contracts which have just expired.

Union involved

The classification by union involved shows if a trade union has been directly involved in the stoppages and describes its affiliation to, in the main, the AFL–CIO (The American Federation of Labor–Confederation of Industrial Organisations), the largest trade union confederation. Other categories are: unaffiliated unions; single-firm unions; different affiliations (that is where unions involved in a single dispute do not have the same affiliation); professional employee associations; and no union involved. For the largest stoppages (those involving 10,000 or more workers) details are given of the individual unions involved where applicable.

Cross–classifications

The following extensive range of cross-classifications are given for the measures 'stoppages', 'workers involved', 'working days lost' in each case:

    X size (measured in number of workers involved) X duration
        stoppages involving 10,000 or more workers X detailed analysis
        including establishment, location, union involved, terms of
        settlement, etc.
    X industry group X size
    X affiliation of labor organisation involved
    X contract status X size
    X industry X contract status
    X contract status X cause (broad groupings)
    X cause (detailed groupings)
    X industry X cause (broad groupings)
    X cause X size
    X industry (detailed classification)
    X industry X occupation

   X cause X level of government (i.e. federal, state, county, city
     or special district level)
     in government X cause X union participation
     in government X occupation X level of government
     in government X function (e.g. welfare services, education, etc.)
   X occupation
     in government X state X union affiliation X recognition
   X state X occupation
   X states having twenty-five stoppages or more X industry
   X industry X duration
   X cause X duration
   X contract status X duration
   X contract status X mediation (level and degree)
   X contract status X type of settlement
   X cause X type of settlement
   X industry X type of settlement
   X contract status X procedure for handling unsettled issues.

Availability of the information

The main statistical series are published by the BLS. A weekly
information sheet is compiled listing those stoppages involving
1,000 workers or more and providing full details of the current
strike situation. This provides the basic information for the monthly
press release which shows, through commentary and statistics,
the current situation in broad detail.

The main publications to contain comprehensive analyses of
stoppages during the year are the *Work Stoppages Summary* (which
appears each July after the year end) and the much more detailed
Analysis of Work Stoppages which takes approximately fifteen
months to appear (each March) but which contains the revisions
to the preliminary figures first issued in the *Summary*. For work
stoppages in government a separate summary appears annually,
and for certain other groups of the labour force separate, *ad hoc*
bulletins might be published.

From the date of the changeover to recording only those stoppages involving 1,000 workers or more (January 1982), monthly
details will be carried in the publication *Current Wage Developments*
and certain of the detailed publications dealing specifically with
stoppages will be discontinued.

Notes

1. For a full discussion of the trend and composition of strikes during the period since 1880 see P. K. Edwards, *Strikes in the United States 1881-1974* (Oxford, Basil Blackwell, 1981).
2. For coverage of this early period in US strike statistics see *Strikes in the United States, 1880 to 1936*, BLS, Bulletin 651 (1938).
3. Figures from *Work Stoppages in Government 1980*, BLS, Bulletin 2110 (October 1981). This is an annual publication specifically covering government disputes.

Table 12.1 USA Summary statistics

	1972	1973	1974	1975	1976	1977	1978	1979	1980	1981
Stoppages	8,382	8,873	10,539	8,897	10,089	9,971	8,120	9,258	7,814	2,781
— Beginning in year	5,010	5,353	6,074	5,031	5,648	5,506	4,230	4,827	3,885	2,568
— Carried over	3,372	3,520	4,465	3,866	4,441	4,465	3,890	4,431	3,929	213
Workers involved (000s)	3,070	3,321	4,560	2,906	3,961	3,327	3,182	3,050	2,657	1,130
— Due to stoppages beginning in year	1,714	2,251	2,778	1,746	2,420	2,040	1,623	1,727	1,366	1,081
— Due to stoppages carried over	1,356	1,070	1,782	1,160	1,541	1,287	1,559	1,323	1,291	49
Working days lost (000s)	27,066	27,948	47,991	31,237	37,859	35,822	36,922	34,754	33,289	24,730

Source: Analysis of Work Stoppages, US Bureau of Labor Statistics.

Table 12.2 USA Working days lost by standard federal regions* (000s)

	1972	1973	1974	1975	1976	1977	1978	1979	1980	1981
Region I	1,007.0	1,542.8	1,538.1	2,595.3	1,687.8	1,076.3	929.9	1,933.2	1,258.0	1,216.0
Region II	5,534.2	2,707.3	2,511.4	3,267.3	3,323.1	1,850.1	2,639.3	3,059.7	2,180.3	1,416.8
Region III	3,909.3	4,327.6	7,257.9	5,569.1	5,208.4	6,620.3	9,181.7	4,452.7	2,947.7	8,485.7
Region IV	2,035.2	2,762.5	5,470.0	2,518.3	4,930.7	4,406.9	4,736.9	3,808.0	2,136.0	2,358.3
Region V	8,272.4	8,120.9	13,792.6	7,567.9	12,624.9	11,646.0	11,395.8	12,495.2	10,240.4	6,999.4
Region VI	1,661.2	2,384.3	2,482.9	4,538.5	1,704.6	1,452.2	1,478.3	1,691.6	2,957.1	941.5
Region VII	1,106.2	1,677.0	3,462.4	2,117.7	2,987.5	2,086.3	1,065.4	1,920.9	880.5	553.1
Region VIII	466.4	316.9	744.4	548.2	204.4	654.5	596.6	465.6	1,139.2	829.8
Region IX	2,483.0	2,942.5	7,781.5	1,895.7	3,246.4	3,963.2	2,756.6	3,858.8	8,202.8	1,563.2
Region X	591.3	1,166.6	2,949.7	619.0	1,941.1	2,066.0	2,141.0	1,068.0	1,346.5	365.9
USA Total	27,066.4	27,948.4	47,990.9	31,237.0	37,858.9	35,821.8	36,921.5	34,753.7	33,288.5	24,729.7

*For constituent states of each region see page 140–1.
Source: Analysis of Work Stoppages, US Bureau of Labor Statistics.

Table 12.3 USA Working days lost by industry* (000s)

	1972	1973	1974	1975	1976	1977	1978	1979	1980	1981
1. Ordinance and accessories	266.8	222.2	153.2	193.7	42.1	46.3	88.1	175.0	–	–
2. Food and kindred products	1,282.9	1,007.9	1,539.1	838.4	1,848.0	1,501.4	558.2	968.7	810.3	314.5
3. Tobacco manufactures	1.8	–	68.2	–	3.2	167.6	1.0	0.5	–	5.4
4. Textile mill products	107.0	268.0	756.4	27.3	115.0	86.4	341.3	193.8	165.1	53.7
5. Apparel and other products	694.0	999.4	893.2	109.5	230.5	182.7	136.7	230.1	61.6	86.3
6. Lumber and wood products	211.1	248.6	332.4	282.6	429.4	340.7	270.9	288.7	419.5	102.0
7. Furniture and fixtures	229.4	290.9	309.0	354.4	266.6	202.8	297.2	272.0	310.0	89.7
8. Paper and allied products	273.3	410.3	685.2	622.2	479.0	507.8	2,177.5	1,135.3	634.3	284.6
9. Printing, publishing etc.	271.7	281.1	545.0	237.6	225.4	241.2	794.3	216.5	131.9	136.8
10. Chemicals and allied products	726.6	501.1	1,599.8	747.4	1,116.8	636.0	632.6	1,172.2	469.3	450.0
11. Petroleum refining and re-lated	126.8	536.8	148.1	613.3	19.1	172.3	88.0	259.8	3,763.5	128.9
12. Rubber and plastics	272.4	1,743.0	971.1	238.1	6,082.4	343.4	362.0	767.9	241.9	101.9
13. Leather and leather products	45.8	22.7	122.8	9.3	55.1	259.0	42.8	163.3	41.8	12.0
14. Stone, clay and glass products	376.0	629.5	1,003.9	484.3	612.5	987.8	469.1	573.7	359.1	271.5
15. Primary metal industries	1,310.9	760.5	1,585.9	1,168.9	1,304.3	2,166.8	1,377.6	1,480.8	3,103.7	886.7
16. Fabricated metal products	1,122.4	1,239.9	2,101.9	1,779.3	1,631.5	1,466.0	1,682.7	1,962.6	1,400.3	725.3

[*Table 12.3 cont. overleaf*]

Table 12.3 (*cont.*)

	1972	1973	1974	1975	1976	1977	1978	1979	1980	1981
17. Machinery except electrical	2,287.8	2,006.4	3,026.1	2,370.8	2,721.8	3,266.9	2,159.7	5,618.1	2,759.1	883.2
18. Electrical machinery etc.	695.4	1,234.2	3,643.0	850.7	2,235.5	1,076.3	1,209.5	2,028.3	753.4	557.8
19. Transportation equipment	1,734.2	1,437.9	3,739.3	3,404.9	4,322.9	4,175.5	2,447.2	2,332.6	2,679.2	930.6
20. Professional and scientific equipment, etc.	134.3	278.3	165.3	287.9	128.1	216.4	289.6	249.1	202.1	76.8
21. Miscellaneous manufacturing	111.9	200.0	209.7	255.6	393.9	288.1	175.8	202.4	204.6	33.9
22. Agriculture, forestry, fisheries	90.9	479.0	459.7	35.9	13.9	23.7	35.4	568.9	107.6	30.6
23. Mining	724.3	865.4	4,061.0	1,642.8	2,220.1	7,280.5	10,260.6	510.8	594.9	8,866.4
24. Contract construction	7,843.7	3,658.0	12,721.0	7,307.3	3,239.8	3,284.4	2,271.8	1,646.4	4,752.5	4,440.4
25. Transport and communication	3,245.0	3,296.5	3,225.5	3,089.0	3,461.3	2,157.1	4,452.5	5,642.7	1,740.7	639.8
26. Wholesale and retail trade	1,131.6	2,123.6	1,757.8	1,426.0	1,311.3	1,988.0	1,757.9	1,368.3	1,402.7	668.9
27. Finance, insurance, real estate	52.7	80.2	62.9	169.0	273.0	96.6	133.4	71.5	54.7	131.2
28. Services	438.4	822.5	700.1	486.6	1,383.6	889.8	701.2	1,671.3	3,776.8	1,215.9
29. Government	1,257.3	2,303.9	1,404.2	2,204.4	1,690.7	1,765.7	1,706.7	2,982.5	2,347.8	2,604.8
All industries and services	27,066.4	27,948.4	47,990.9	31,237.0	37,858.9	35,821.8	36,921.5	34,753.7	33,288.5	24,729.7

*Due to rounding, the sum of constituent items may not agree with totals.
Source: Analysis of Work Stoppages, US Bureau of Labor Statistics.

Table 12.4 USA Working days lost by cause* (000s)

	1972	1973	1974	1975	1976	1977	1978	1979	1980	1981
General wage claims	17,094.3	16,714.6	38,924.4	22,221.7	23,778.6	21,694.8	19,341.4	25,640.0	22,020.2	20,973.8
Supplementary benefits	569.2	1,067.2	1,104.3	277.8	189.0	453.5	271.8	659.7	294.4	496.4
Wage adjustments	330.6	400.4	445.2	364.3	562.0	1,625.3	581.2	1,334.7	2,361.1	156.2
Hours of work	4.6	13.5	443.8	9.8	56.9	84.8	261.0	26.1	14.0	5.1
Other contractual matters	1,540.8	639.1	818.6	405.8	338.0	1,350.7	721.1	786.8	875.7	292.0
Union organisation and security	2,280.7	3,378.4	1,841.4	1,488.0	2,454.9	955.0	762.4	1,118.8	672.6	389.3
Job security	1,243.4	2,445.4	1,543.0	3,153.6	7,186.9	1,708.9	4,027.3	2,460.9	3,497.6	1,713.5
Plant administration	3,450.3	2,770.5	2,340.8	2,883.7	2,776.6	7,249.2	10,612.4	2,490.1	3,327.1	588.7
Other working conditions	227.7	167.4	256.4	197.9	178.1	338.8	181.8	120.0	99.2	72.3
Inter/Intra-union matters	279.1	314.9	188.1	200.9	288.2	335.4	152.3	97.0	79.0	39.9
Not reported	45.8	37.2	84.7	33.5	49.5	25.4	8.7	19.6	47.6	2.3
All stoppages	27,066.4	27,948.4	47,990.9	31,237.0	37,858.9	35,821.8	36,921.5	34,753.7	33,288.5	24,729.7

*Due to rounding, the sum of constituent items may not agree with totals.
Source: Analysis of Work Stoppages, US Bureau of Labor Statistics.

PART III

PATTERNS OF STOPPAGE ACTIVITY

13 GENERAL PATTERNS OF ACTIVITY, 1972-81

The first chapter in this part of the book examines the observed pattern of stoppage activity drawn from the available statistics and using the four main measures of activity—number of stoppages, establishments affected, workers involved and working days lost. Previous chapters have already pointed to the serious problems to be encountered in using the national statistics for international comparisons and these will be referred to as necessary when examining the data in this and the succeeding three chapters. However, it would be wrong if such inconsistencies precluded all international comparisons of stoppage activity since, when used carefully, they can show much about relative experiences and hence provide valuable background information for a better understanding of many other measures of economic performance such as productivity, for example.

Despite the obvious interest in comparative performance, there is relatively little previous work which examines in detail the different patterns of stoppage activity across countries. Apart from the few studies which have looked at the problem of data comparability as well as the statistical trends,[1] and which have already been mentioned, the main body of work on the subject is now quite dated. In particular the studies by Kerr and Siegal[2] and Ross and Hartman[3] are particularly old, and the works by Turner[4] and McCarthy[5] cover the periods prior to the seventies decade and are only of limited value in the somewhat different economic climate of the eighties.

Much of the use of national statistics on stoppages of work for international comparisons is focused on the regular publication of data by national bodies such as the Department of Employment in the UK and the Statistisches Bundesamt in Germany in their regular publications.[6] Otherwise it is the supranational organisations such as the ILO and the EEC who use the statistics in their regular publications, covering many headings of economic data in addition to stoppages.[7] In all such cases, however, the information is usually confined to the simple presentation of the data without any detailed commentary on trends.

The reasons for this dearth of comparative international work are not clear. Certainly a major factor will be the significant problems in methods of collection and definitions applied to the statistics of each country, which in many cases cast doubt on the validity of using the data for such purposes. Further, the significant differences lying behind the statistics, in the causes of strikes and lockouts, may be another factor discouraging international comparisons. If a country's stoppages record is influenced by the structure of its industrial relations machinery, for example, then is it fair to compare stoppages in countries with different industrial relations structures? In such cases it might be argued that the comparison of stoppage statistics will reflect rather the differences in the established machinery for resolving disputes than the propensity to take such action. The influence of industrial relations practices on stoppage activity is discussed more fully in Chapter 16.

Whatever the cause of the lack of detailed international comparisons, provided that the statistics are used selectively and interpreted in the correct way, then there is every reason to compare across countries. With this in mind, the remainder of this chapter discusses the statistics over the ten-year period 1972–81 for the nine countries covered in this study, illustrating not only the observed broader patterns of activity, but also how the statistics should be used, given the differences in methods of collection and definitions.

Main measures of activity

The basic pattern of industrial disputes will tend to vary from year to year and will be subject to a variety of influences, many of which will be exogenously determined. Foremost among these external influences will be the prevailing labour market conditions as proxied by the unemployment rate, for example. In other words, if the level of unemployment is seen to increase relatively, then workers will tend to be less keen to take strike action given that it may threaten their continued employment.

The effects of such external factors on strike propensity have been well documented for individual countries by, for example, Edwards for the USA[8] and Smith et al. for the UK,[9] and many of the findings will be broadly applicable to other countries. Of the international studies carried out in this area, the work of Clark is worth mentioning.[10] Here the author compared the stoppage activity in six countries, three displaying relatively low activity (one of which was Germany) and three where stoppage activity was considerably higher (one of which was Italy). He found that there was some positive association between a high level of strike activity and comparatively high levels of inflation and unemployment. Creigh *et al.* also concluded that there was a 'statistically significant' association between the incidence of stoppages (as measured by working days lost per 1,000 workers) and price inflation and unemployment in the twenty OECD countries they examined.[11] However, it is not possible to generalise about these findings without bringing into question the results from the statistical analyses. All the studies used the readily available data, with the associated problems of compatibility.

In an effort to overcome the problem of annual fluctuations in stoppage activity which make it unreliable to take the statistics from just one or two years as a guide to overall levels of activity, the figures in Table 13.1 are annual averages for the ten-year period 1972-81. The figures in the table show that the experience of the nine countries differed considerably according to the recorded data, but then this would be expected, particularly when comparing countries with labour forces of different sizes. Thus the bland figures in Table 13.1 convey little useful information that could provide the basis for international comparisons of relative stoppages of work experience. To achieve this, the basic figures need to be adjusted for labour force size.

Nevertheless, there is one interesting statistic that can be derived from Table 13.1 involving the three countries that measure both the number of stoppages and establishments affected, namely Belgium, France and Ireland. From this information it is possible to derive a crude measure of the number of establishments affected per stoppage on average over the period. So, in the case of Belgium this works out at 2.6 establishments per stoppage, with corresponding figures for France of 7.1 and Ireland of 1.3. The wide differences between, on the one hand, Belgium and Ireland, and on the other France, is strictly a function of the relative size (in employment terms) of each country. Basically, in most industrial sectors, France will have more individual plants with larger associated labour forces and this will mean that single stoppages will tend to affect more individual establishments.

In order to reflect the different relative sizes of the labour forces in each country the main measures of activity need to be expressed in terms of numbers of workers.[12] Table 13.2 shows the variation in the size of labour forces for 1980 across the nine countries. The considerably large variations in size of labour force emphasise the limited explanative use of the basic stoppage statistics without the appropriate adjustment. Therefore, Table 13.3 takes the three main measures of number of stoppages, workers involved and working

Table 13.1 Main measures compared (annual averages 1972-81)

	Number of stoppages	Establishments affected	Workers involved	Working days lost
Belgium*	209	537	74,770	645,579
Denmark	180	†	100,118	578,740
France	3,447	24,631	1,480,210	3,262,230
Germany	†	514	156,070	725,559
Ireland	153	205	34,772	541,564
Italy	3,224	†	10,523,600	17,168,100
Netherlands	28	†	19,551	136,450
UK	2,280	†	1,552,800	12,040,300
USA	8,723	†	3,116,400	33,761,800

*Annual average for 1972-80 only.
†Figures not available.
Source: National statistics.

Table 13.2 The size of labour forces 1980

	Labour force (000s)
Belgium	3,751
Denmark	2,470
France	21,142
Germany	25,265
Ireland	1,148
Italy	20,572
Netherlands	4,669
UK	24,367
USA	99,303

Source: Labour Force Statistics (OECD).

days lost and expresses each in terms of the size of the employed labour force, giving the annual averages for the period 1972-81. Taking the number of stoppages per 100,000 workers first, the table shows that the highest incidence was recorded by France and Italy, both with seventeen stoppages per 100,000 workers over the period 1972-81. At the other extreme, the lowest incidence was recorded by the Netherlands with only one stoppage per 100,000 workers. There is no doubt that the corresponding figure for Germany would be equally low if it were available. However, separate statistics

Table 13.3 Main measures by labour force size (annual averages 1972-81)

	Stoppages per 100,000 workers	Workers involved per 1,000 workers	Working days lost per 1,000 workers
Belgium*	6	20	173
Denmark	8	42	241
France	17	71	156
Germany	†	6	29
Ireland	14	32	496
Italy	17	528	870
Netherlands	1	4	30
UK	9	64	492
USA	9	35	371

*Annual average for 1972–80 only.
†Figures not available.
Note: For Belgium, Denmark, Ireland and the Netherlands, in the absence of estimates of labour force size for 1981, the 1980 figures have been applied for that year.
Source: National statistics and *Labour Force Statistics* (OECD).

on the number of stoppages are not compiled (for further details see Chapter 7).

The second measure, the number of workers involved in stoppages per 1,000 workers, tells something of the proportion of all employees affected by disputes. Caution is necessary, however, since the statistics are inevitably affected by cases where one worker is involved with a number of individual disputes over a given period. Therefore, the basic figures cannot be taken simply as the proportion of the total in exact terms. Unfortunately, from the available statistics it is impossible to unravel the extent of this multiple involvement, so the statistics can at best provide only an indication of the proportion of all workers affected by stoppages.

By far the highest proportion is shown to be Italy with a figure of 528 workers involved in stoppages per 1,000 workers overall. This figure is way ahead of all the other countries which record at the most seventy-one workers involved, being the case of France. The lowest figures are those for the Netherlands with four workers and Germany with six workers involved on average over the ten-year period. This measure does indicate the widespread effects of stoppages on workers in Italy compared to the remaining countries and to a great extent is a function of the types of stoppage common in that country.

In Italy, there has been a tendency towards the use of stoppages of short duration but involving large numbers of workers. Many of these are protest strikes, some with a political flavour and therefore cutting across a number of industrial sectors. For example, over the ten-year period 1972–81, Italy experienced an average worker involvement of 3,264 workers per recorded stoppage, compared to a similar figure of only 698 for the Netherlands or 681 for the UK.[13]

The comparative statistics will also be affected by the inclusion or exclusion of indirect effects in particular and the treatment of other types of stoppage in general (as discussed in Chapter 3). This problem will be particularly acute in the case of France, Germany and Italy where indirect effects are not measured. So there is even the likelihood that the Italian figure, as high as it is, is nevertheless an underestimate of actual numbers affected.

However, the most significant comparative measure of activity is the number of working days lost as a result of all recorded disputes. The reasons for this have already been explained in Chapter 3, but mainly rest on the fact that it will be the one main measure of activity the least affected by the application of a minimum size threshold under which disputes are not counted.

The statistics in Table 13.3 show working days lost per 1,000 workers. In the case of Italy the unit of recording is hours rather than days and hence they have been converted into the latter by application of a simple divisor of eight representing an eight-hour day. Given the fact that the number of normal hours worked has tended to move downwards for most occupations in Italy over the period 1972–81, the estimate of days lost is at best a slight underestimate of the actual normal working days lost. Apart from the special case of Italy, however, the other countries should have statistics which are reasonably comparable, with more or less common differences.

Applying a basic ranking to the nine countries reveals that the worst record is that for Italy with an average of 870 days lost for every 1,000 workers over the ten-year period. This is way ahead of the nearest contenders for the top position, Ireland and the UK, with 496 days lost and 492 days lost per 1,000 workers respectively. The order then consists of the USA (371), Denmark (241), Belgium (173) and France (156), with the best record of the nine in the Netherlands (30) and Germany (29).

To some extent the differences between the countries, particularly between those at the top and bottom of the ranking, is a result of the different measurement systems and definitions applied to the statistics. It is certainly the case that the three countries with the worst records—Italy, Ireland and the UK—have relatively good measurement systems, though significantly Italy excludes the measurement of indirect effects and the UK any political stoppages. On the other hand, both the Netherlands and Germany, those countries with the best comparative record, have well established measurement systems and although the German statistics exclude indirect effects, any political stoppages are included (though, in fact, are probably rare in practice). In the case of the Netherlands, there is the minimum of restrictions with, in effect, all stoppages being included provided that the central statistical agency learns of their occurrence.

In short, therefore, the sometimes exceptionally large differences in working days lost per 1,000 workers over the period 1972-81 must be the result of more than just differences in measurement and definition. There is clearly a vastly different experience of industrial disputes in most of the countries, which is accounted for largely by the propensity to strike shown by workers in each country which, in turn, is conditioned by such factors as trade union power, historical precedent and, more importantly, the existence of industrial relations practices which enable disputes to be resolved before the strike or lockout is resorted to.

The trend of activity

In many ways the use of average annual statistics can mask the more interesting comparisons of trends of activity over a long period of time. The comparison of trends in stoppage activity is the least problematic of all international comparisons of such data since, on the whole, measurement systems and definitions have changed little over the past ten years. There have been some changes, but with a few exceptions these have been relatively subtle. The exceptions include, for example, the case of Italy where political strikes were excluded from the statistics prior to 1975 (see Chapter 9). As a result the statistics from 1975 onwards will tend to be at a higher overall level than those prior to the year of the changeover, assuming a significant incidence of political protest strikes (which is a fair assumption to make in the case of Italy). In most cases, though, the trend statistics can be relied on.

The use of the least contentious measure of activity, working days lost per 1,000 workers, combined with national time series statistics, should produce reasonably accurate results. Such statistics have been used to derive the curves in Figures 13.1 to 13.9 each plotting the national trend over the period 1972-81 in most cases. Based on the

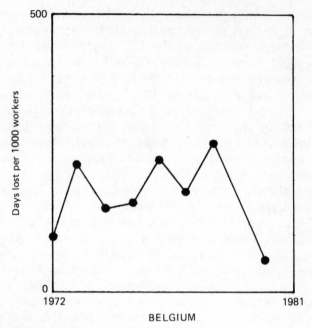

Figure 13.1 The trend of working days lost in Belgium

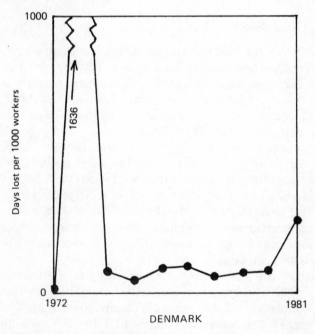

Figure 13.2 The trend of working days lost in Denmark

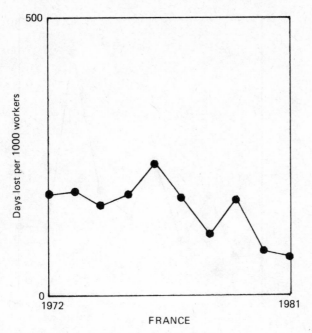

Figure 13.3 The trend of working days lost in France

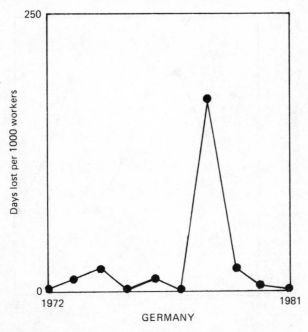

Figure 13.4 The trend of working days lost in Germany

Figure 13.5 The trend of working days lost in Ireland

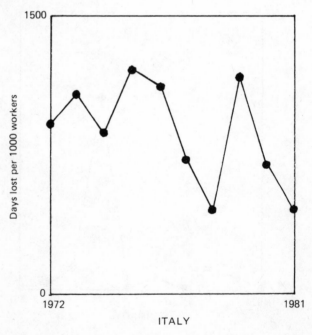

Figure 13.6 The trend of working days lost in Italy

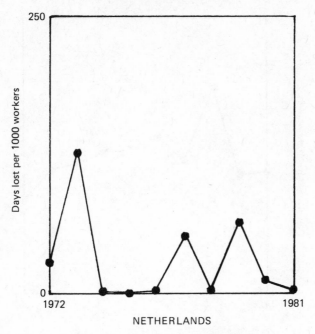

Figure 13.7 The trend of working days lost in the Netherlands

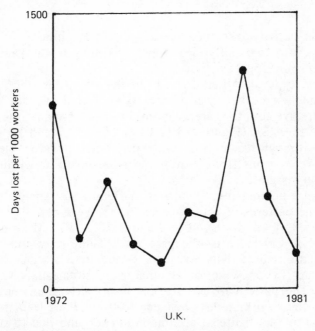

Figure 13.8 The trend of working days lost in the UK

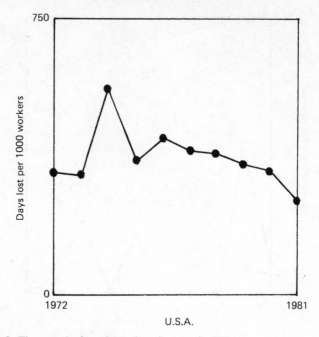

Figure 13.9 The trend of working days lost in the USA

patterns of activity displayed in the graphs, the nine countries can be divided into two fairly clear types according to the year-to-year fluctuations in stoppage activity.

The first type identified consists of five countries who generally show a much smoother level of activity measured over the ten-year period. The five countries are Belgium, France, Germany, the Netherlands, and the USA (Figures 13.1, 13.3, 13.4, 13.7 and 13.9 respectively). Although each country experienced different levels of activity, fluctuations from year to year tended to be within a relatively small margin.

For the remaining four countries of Denmark, Ireland, Italy and the UK, the patterns of activity over the ten-year period are significantly different (as displayed in Figures 13.2, 13.5, 13.6 and 13.8 respectively). Certainly in the case of Ireland, Italy and the UK, the fluctuations in activity over the period have been both violent and regular. In the case of Denmark the situation is somewhat different. The pattern of activity has been fairly consistent except for 1973 when working days lost per 1,000 workers leapt to 1,636, the highest annual figure of all nine countries, and due to an exceptionally high level of stoppages affecting most industrial sectors (see Table 5.2). In many ways this was an aberration and apart from this year the Danish record shows a fairly smooth pattern.

The importance of the trend in stoppages of work in each country is fairly clear. If the general propensity to take strike action is volatile, then it is difficult to predict the likely level of activity over a period. Predictability is always a useful thing to both the economic and corporate planner alike. In addition, the fluctuations in strike activity could create the wrong impression to prospective foreign or even national investors, who may prefer a location with a fairly uniform trend of stoppage activity.

Recently there has been another aspect to the interest in the trend of stoppages of work and this relates to the effects of economic recession on the level of such activity. It has been consistently argued that the decision to strike, as taken by workers or their representatives, is strongly influenced by external factors such as the level of unemployment as well as by the more obvious internal motivations. All nine countries examined in this study have experienced recession of different severities from approximately 1979 onwards and so there should be some observable falling off in stoppage activity from about this year, if the theory as outlined above is to hold true.

Looking at the pattern of working days lost per 1,000 workers as portrayed in Figures 13.1 to 13.9 for each country, in most cases there has been a noticeable decline in the measure from about 1979. In the UK, for example, the number of working days lost per 1,000 workers over a ten-year period reached a peak in 1979 with 1,190 days lost. By 1981 the corresponding figure was a mere 175 days lost. Ireland and Italy have shown similar pronounced declines and although in the remaining countries the levelling off of stoppage activity is less dramatic, there seems to be this dampening down effect of the recession. The one exception to this trend is Denmark, where over 1979–81, working days lost increased overall, with a particularly sharp increase between 1980 and 1981. However, given the peculiar problems of the Danish system of recording stoppages, this may not be a completely reliable result.

The relationship between recession and a lower level of stoppage activity is, on the face of it, a fairly obvious one. In a situation of high unemployment, employed workers will have less bargaining power—given an employer's freedom to sack striking workers, of course, which may not always be the case. An existing pool of alternative labour as represented by the unemployed will mean that existing employees could be easily replaced. Consequently, these factors will figure strongly in the workers' decision to strike.

Stoppages in perspective

Despite the degree of interest accorded stoppages of work in most of the countries, it is important that they should be seen in the context of their overall contribution to the amount of working time lost due to all causes.

In Chapter 1, it was explained that strikes and lockouts constitute only two types of the more broadly defined concept of stoppages of work. Other types of industrial action such as go-slows, work-to-rules and overtime bans all contribute to lost production. In addition the other interruptions to normal working which are not, at least in most cases, the direct result of a labour dispute, such as lateness and absenteeism, add further to the total amount of output lost over a period of time.

In a country with a comparatively low recorded level of stoppage activity, therefore, such as France over the period 1972–81, the contribution of such activity to the total amount of lost production from all causes is going to be small. Kennedy reports that a study of the year 1975 showed that absenteeism in French industry accounted for about 100 times the number of days lost through strikes.[14] Even in a country where the recorded level of stoppages is considerably higher, as in the case of Italy for example, the same author reports that over the ten-year period 1967–76 less than 1 per cent of production was lost due to strikes, while about 8 per cent was lost due solely to absenteeism due to sickness.[15]

The best figures, however, are those available on the USA and published regularly by the Bureau of Labor Statistics. These figures show the percentage of estimated total working time accounted for by stoppages over a year. Therefore, taking the period 1972–81, the annual figures are given in Table 13.4. The statistics show that the maximum percentage over the ten-year period reached only 0.24 per cent in 1974 and generally the figure was much lower with an annual average of 0.16 per cent.

Clearly then, in those countries with very low recorded levels of stoppage activity, such as Germany and the Netherlands, the contribution of stoppages to lost production will tend to be negligible. It is in this context that strikes and lockouts should be seen; and it may even be correct to talk of an optimal level of stoppage activity below which it would be unrealistic to expect a country to fall. Determining this level of activity, however, is probably an impossible task.

Table 13.4 The contribution of stoppages to total lost working time in the USA, 1972-81

	% of estimated total working time lost due to stoppages
1972	0.15
1973	0.14
1974	0.24
1975	0.16
1976	0.19
1977	0.17
1978	0.17
1979	0.15
1980	0.14
1981	0.11

Source: *Analysis of Work Stoppages* (US, Bureau of Labor Statistics).

Notes

1. The main studies are Fisher, M., *Measurement of Labour Disputes and their Economic Effects* (Paris, OECD, 1973); Creigh, S., Donaldson, N. and Hawthorn, E., 'Stoppage activity in OECD countries', *Employment Gazette* (November 1980); and Walsh, K., 'An analysis of strikes in four EEC countries', *Industrial Relations Journal* Vol 13:4 (Winter 1982).
2. Kerr, C. and Siegel, A., 'The inter-industry propensity to strike—international comparison', in Kornhauser, A., Dubin, R. and Ross, A. M., *Industrial Conflict* (New York, McGraw-Hill, 1954).
3. Ross, A. M. and Hartman, P. T., *Changing Patterns of Industrial Conflict* (New York, Wiley, 1960).
4. Turner, H. A., *Is Britain Really Strike Prone?* (Cambridge, Cambridge University Press, 1969).
5. McCarthy, W. E. J., 'The nature of Britain's strike problem', *British Journal of Industrial Relations*, Vol. 8 (1970).
6. In the case of the UK, the international statistics appear annually in the *Employment Gazette* (London, HMSO). In Germany, there is a special issue of the publication *Statistik des Auslandes, Reihe 1.3, Streiks und Aussperrungen in Ausland* (Weisbaden, Statistiches Bundesamt).
7. The ILO publishes details of stoppages in certain member countries in its publication *Yearbook of Labour Statistics* (Geneva, ILO, annually). The EEC figures are published in *Employment and Unemployment* (Luxembourg, Eurostat, annually).

8. Edwards, P. K., *Strikes in the United States 1881–1974* (Oxford, Basil Blackwell, 1981).

9. Smith, C. T. B., Clifton, R., Makeham, P., Creigh, S. W. and Burn, R. V., *Strikes in Britain* (London, HMSO, DE Manpower Paper No. 15, 1978).

10. Clark, O., 'Labour Management disputes: a perspective', *British Journal of Industrial Relations*, Vol. 18:1 (March 1980).

11. Reported in a technical appendix to Creigh, S., Donaldson, N. and Hawthorn, E., op. cit. See also the article by S. Creigh, 'Strikes in OECD countries', *Industrial Relations Journal*, Vol. 13:3 (Autumn 1982).

12. Labour force in this context is taken to be the civilian employed labour force or basically those with the ability to either take strike action or be locked out of their place of work. The figures basically exclude those in the armed forces, but since in all nine countries the armed forces are prohibited from taking strike action, this limited definition is appropriate.

13. See the appropriate national tables in Part II for the statistics used to derive this measure.

14. Kennedy, T., *European Labor Relations* (Lexington, D. C. Heath, 1980), p. 56.

15. Ibid., p. 95.

14   CAUSE AND DURATION OF STOPPAGES

Analysis of the reasons why strikes or lockouts happen is a complex area of study. Certainly it is true that in most cases the occurrence of a work stoppage of this sort is an indication that there is a rift between workers and management which has not been solved through the normal channels of communication. This explains the majority of incidences, but will not cover those political protest or sympathetic stoppages, for example where management may not be directly involved in the cause of the stoppage though is naturally affected by it.

In many ways, however, knowledge of the cause of a stoppage can provide a good deal of information about other characteristics, in particular its duration or potential length. Take the case of a strike called for ostensibly political reasons, perhaps a protest at the proposed introduction of a particular piece of legislation. In all the countries covered in this study that count such strikes, the indications are that they will be usually of short duration, one day or less being the common length. In this example, the cause of the stoppage has indicated (albeit from past experience of such stoppages) the likely duration of it.

Of course, the link between cause and duration can be quite tenuous, particularly in the face of other factors which can influence how long a stoppage will last for. Foremost amongst these must be the amount of financial compensation available to those on strike, either coming from union funds or from state social security payments. Whatever finance is available, the likelihood is that it will amount to considerably less than that which would normally be received from wages, and as such could be a determinant in the length of time a stoppage lasts.[1] In the case of Italy, for example, strikers would be unlikely to receive any financial help since generally they are not eligible for unemployment benefits whilst on strike and the unions on the whole do not pay any strike benefits.

This chapter examines the classifications of stoppage data by cause and duration in those countries of the nine which actually collect and publish usable statistics on them. There will also be some further discussion of the possible link between cause and duration towards the end of the chapter.

Causes of stoppages

There has been much discussion of the value of a classification of stoppages by cause. Such analyses inevitably depend on the sometimes arbitrary grouping of what are probably a multiplicity of causes, all or some of which happen to come together at a point in time and cause a strike (or lockout in some isolated cases). In fact, McCarthy has argued that to call such a classification the 'cause' of a stoppage is something of a misnomer.[2] Realistically, he argues, it is more a listing of the 'principal reasons' given by those involved in the dispute at the time of the stoppage. Invariably, given the methods of data collection used in all nine countries examined here, these will be the reasons as perceived by management.

Clearly then, the analyses by cause of dispute will only reflect the ostensible reason for the dispute and may mask the more accurate (and more interesting) underlying reasons. In particular, it could be argued that the very occurrence of a strike is a reflection of the state of labour–management relations in the establishment, or more broadly, the lack or failure of the conditions in which, if present, a dispute could be resolved before it reaches the stage of strike action.

This underlines a fundamental problem in international comparisons of the causes of disputes, that is, how to take account of the different attitudes and formal facilities prevalent in each country which influence the timing of the decision to take strike action. The context of industrial relations practices is discussed more fully in Chapter 16, but at this stage the possible implications of such differences should be considered in the discussion of cause and duration.

A further complication in international comparisons arises from the fact that only six of the nine countries actually produce classifications by cause. In addition, each classification is basically different though there are some common causes listed. The classifications in the six countries of Belgium, Ireland, Italy, the Netherlands, the UK and the USA, permit only a limited degree of comparison, with the broad cause of 'wage issues' being the most suitable for this purpose.

The statistics for these six countries over the ten years 1972–81 are shown in Table 14.1. The classification for the Netherlands is, in particular, somewhat narrow compared with the other five countries having only four categories, two of which are related to pay questions, the third covering issues concerned with working conditions and

Table 14.1 Working days lost due to wage disputes (percentage of all working days lost)

	Belgium	Ireland	Italy	Netherlands	UK	USA
1972	89.1	47.0	20.5	8.3	*	63.2
1973	84.8	35.8	14.8	99.8	72.0	59.8
1974	83.3	26.7	61.8	55.8	88.3	81.1
1975	78.4	45.9	40.9	–	75.2	71.1
1976	68.8	78.6	7.3	98.2	52.2	62.8
1977	73.9	46.3	21.2	99.4	79.2	60.6
1978	14.0	65.8	18.7	68.2	78.9	52.3
1979	20.6	96.0	8.3	96.0	93.4	73.8
1980	28.1	60.4	10.8	*	88.7	66.1
1981	*	48.9	*	*	62.0	84.8
Annual average	60.1	55.1	22.7	65.7	76.7	67.6

*Figures not available.
Source: National statistics.

the fourth with protest strikes. However, even with a relatively straightforward comparison of working days lost through wage disputes, there is a need for caution. In particular, the Italian figures (which are drawn from that country's fairly detailed classification by cause, see Table 9.4) are probably an understatement of the amount of working time lost due to wage issues. This is because Italy's classification includes a category covering those stoppages caused by the renewal of labour contracts. Within this category there will inevitably be a significant proportion of wage issues hidden since discussion of wage increases, for example, often take place at the point of transition to a new contract.

For the other five countries shown in Table 14.1, it is clear that the major reason for stoppages has to do with issues of wages or associated benefits (for example, bonus payments). In Belgium the annual average is 60.1 per cent of all working days lost, in Ireland it amounts to 55.1 per cent, in the Netherlands 65.7 per cent, in the UK 76.7 per cent and in the USA 67.6 per cent. In most of the five countries, the proportions have remained reasonably high throughout the ten-year period, though in the case of Belgium the latest three years shown, 1978–80, have witnessed exceptionally low proportions of working days lost due to pay issues. Similarly in the Netherlands most years have shown a consistently high proportion, except for 1972 when extensive protest stoppages accounted for approximately 84 per cent of all working days lost (see Table 10.5). Table 4.4 gives more specific details for Belgium of the other reasons recorded for this period, but it appears that the main cause there has been attributed to either trade union matters or other causes not identified separately.

The available data in four of the six countries that actually produce a classification by cause enable the extent of sympathetic action to be measured. All four countries—Belgium, Ireland, Italy and the UK—separately identify (where possible) the cases where workers take action to support their fellow workers elsewhere. This type of action specifically tends not to be a reflection of the state of labour–management relations in the striking establishment, since the root cause will lie elsewhere at the original place where the dispute first began.

The available data over the ten-year period 1972–81 is given in annual average form in Table 14.2. In all countries the proportion of all working days lost due to sympathetic action is small, though the gap between Italy with 4.4 per cent and the rest is quite significant. In Belgium the proportion amounts to 1.2 per cent, while in the UK and Ireland the proportions are 0.3 and 0.2 per cent respectively. In the latter three countries, the low proportions are indicative of a low tendency to take action in support of fellow workers which may, at first glance, appear surprising given the frequent claims of union solidarity made in comment on these countries.

Table 14.2 Working days lost due to sympathetic action (annual average percentage of all working days lost classified as sympathetic action, 1972–81)

Belgium*	1.2
Ireland	0.2
Italy†	4.4
UK‡	0.3

*Annual average for 1972–78 only.
†Annual average for 1972–80 only.
‡Annual average for 1972–81 only.
Source: National statistics.

However, understanding the organisation of strikes and how a grievance is turned into mass support for a stoppage of work is a complex area, more in the subject of the sociology of work practices. In this context the work of Batstone et al. is to be commended, for this has contributed significantly to the understanding of the path to a strike call.[3] In particular the authors point to the degree of organisation required for an official strike and the fact that in very few cases do ordinary workers actually initiate action, though they may be at the centre of the dispute in question. The study was confined to one UK case study and so perhaps should not be too widely applied, especially on an international level where national differences in factors such as worker representation and union density play their part in shaping shop floor negotiations, though despite these, there must be significant similarities and common lessons.

Duration of stoppages

The duration of a stoppage is a particularly important measure since it is generally used, along with the number of workers involved, to calculate the amount of working time lost. However, its value goes beyond this simple use as a multiplier since duration can say a good deal about the character and trend of stoppages. For example, it might be expected that the length of time for which a dispute lasts will be a function of factors such as the economic circumstances of the strikers. If they are being financially supported by their union, then there may be less pressure on the strikers to stop their actions or compromise with management. Thus, the duration statistics can indicate if such relationships are actually corroborated by the evidence.

Hyman goes further in describing the importance of measuring duration, suggesting that it can show the differences in two fundamentally different characteristics of industrial action.[4] The first such characteristic is termed 'the trial of strength' and will typically be displayed in stoppages of longer duration than the second and more common 'demonstration stoppage'. The latter will generally be a token demonstration of a grievance, mainly aimed at bringing things to the attention of management rather than the prelude to some bitter, protracted struggle.

Some of the problems in measuring the duration of a stoppage have already been discussed in Chapter 2, but in addition there are significant difficulties to be encountered because of the timing and variable support in different stoppages. All nine countries exclude days not normally worked from their duration calculations (e.g. weekends and statutory holidays), but there still remains the problem of exactly when a strike or lockout starts and finishes—frequently in the middle of a day and not conveniently at the beginning or end—and the variability in the degree of support for it (in terms of workers involved) which, on the whole, is never going to be straightforward to determine whatever system of measurement is used.

Given these basic problems in measuring the duration of a stoppage in each of the nine countries, it is nevertheless necessary for each country to attempt to calculate it for the basic reasons outlined above. However, whether through a lack of confidence in the measure derived or more simply through an imposed limit on the amount of information released, three of the nine countries covered in this study, Denmark, France and Italy, choose not to publish any details of duration. The remaining six countries do produce regular statistics on all or some of the main measures of activity, though inevitably using different duration categories which seriously inhibits any comparative analyses.

Four of the six countries—Ireland, the Netherlands, the UK and the USA—publish reasonably comprehensive statistics on the three main measures of 'stoppages', 'workers involved' and 'working time lost', using their own duration bands (as described in the appropriate national chapters in Part II). Belgium, though using a detailed list of duration bands, limits the statistics to covering just 'stoppages' and 'workers involved'. The narrowest classification, however, is that published by Germany which has only three duration bands (measured in working days lost) and these are only published for 'workers involved'.

The differences in the classifications used by each country are compounded by the variations in both definition and use of a minimum size for inclusion into the statistics (five of the six having such criteria), such that the shorter disputes (usually those lasting less than one working day) are automatically excluded. This will mean that the duration statistics derived for such countries will be seriously deficient at the lowest category of duration. The differences mean that it is both very difficult and, even if possible, somewhat spurious to compile a table of comparable results between the six countries. Consequently, each of them, with the exception of Germany where the range of data available is considered too limited for any effective comparison, is discussed individually below, with some comparative aspects followed up subsequently. Where possible the two main measures of 'stoppages' and 'working days lost' have been used.

Belgium

The proportions of all recorded stoppages in four broad duration bands for Belgium are given in Table 14.3.[5] As with all the statistics on duration used here, they are taken over a number of years and averaged out, this being the most effective way to ensure that one exceptional year is not taken to be typical of other periods.

Table 14.3 Duration of stoppages in Belgium (annual average percentage 1972–78, stoppages beginning in each year)

	Stoppages
Less than 2 days	24.6
2–10 days	49.7
11–30 days	19.5
31 days and over	6.2
All	100.0

Source: *Annuaire Statistique de la Belgique*, Institut National de Statistique.

The statistics show that approximately 24.6 per cent of all recorded stoppages were of less than two working days' duration. However, this is inevitably a serious understatement of the actual number of short stoppages since those lasting less than one day are excluded from the statistics anyway. In common with most other countries, the incidence of short stoppages is comparatively high, though, as already mentioned, in the absence of precise figures on Belgium for those that are excluded, it is not possible to substantiate this observation. The only country of the six that actually records all stoppages coming to the attention of the recording agency and at the same time publishes duration statistics, is the Netherlands. In this country, as Table 14.5 shows, over the period 1973–9, 19.1 per cent of all stoppages lasted less than one day. Therefore, it is probably fair to assume that in Belgium the proportion of unrecorded stoppages because of the application of a minimum size for inclusion, will be of this order.

For the other duration categories, it is clear that they will be overestimates of the proportion·of total stoppages in each. Even so, the largest duration category of thirty-one days and over clearly accounts for a very small proportion of the total number of stoppages, at 6.2 per cent. Unfortunately, Belgium does not publish statistics of working days lost by duration and so it is not possible to estimate the corresponding proportions for working time lost in each category.

Ireland

The statistics on the duration of stoppages in Ireland allow the comparison of both stoppages and the number of working days lost, as shown in Table 14.4, which uses data over the ten-year period 1972–81. For the smallest duration category of one to two days, the limitations mentioned in connection with Belgium, in that those stoppages lasting less than one working day are excluded, are relevant here also. Thus all measures will tend to be over-estimates of the proportions of the total number of stoppages. For working days lost, the discrepancy will only be comparatively small, however, since the short duration stoppages usually only account for a few working days lost in total.

Table 14.4 Duration of stoppages in Ireland (annual average percentage 1972–81, stoppages beginning in each year)

	Stoppages	Working days lost
1–2 days	22.8	2.2
3–10 days	43.8	14.1
11–30 days	21.2	17.2
31 days and over	12.2	66.5
All	100.0	100.0

Source: Irish Statistical Bulletin, Central Statistics Office.

The figures in Table 14.4 show that again the majority of all stoppages were of short duration, over two-thirds lasting less than ten days. However, the interesting part is that this large proportion of stoppages accounted for a significantly disproportionate amount of working days lost, the corresponding figure being only 16.3 per cent. The majority of days lost, around two-thirds of the total, were a result of the 12.2 per cent of stoppages which lasted for thirty-one days or over.

The Netherlands

The relatively low level of stoppage activity over the period 1972–81 in the Netherlands has already been discussed in the previous chapter. The Dutch statistics include all stoppages coming to the attention of the recording agency, the CBS, and so the figures presented in Table 14.5 will be relatively unaffected by any exclusion category. They are only comparatively unaffected, however, because many of the smaller stoppages will escape notification and recording anyway.

Table 14.5 Duration of stoppages in the Netherlands (annual average percentage, 1973-79)

	Stoppages	Working days lost
Less than one day	19.1	1.2
1-5 days	46.0	6.6
5-10 days	13.2	13.0
10 days and over	21.7	79.2
All	100.0	100.0

Source: Sociale Maandstatistiek, Centraal Bureau voor de Statistiek.

The statistics show that 19.1 per cent of all recorded stoppages were under one day's duration, yet these accounted for only 1.2 per cent of all days lost. The majority of disputes lasted for between one and under five days, with a percentage of 46, though again accounting for only a small proportion, 6.6 per cent, of all working days lost.

The majority of days lost, almost four-fifths (or 79.2 per cent) were accounted for by only 21.7 per cent or just over one-fifth of all working days lost. Most of these were accounted for by higher than average levels of stoppage activity in 1973, 1977 and 1979, which leads to the tentative conclusion that during a period when the overall level of activity is higher than usual, it will tend to be reflected in longer, protracted disputes.

The relatively low level of strike activity generally in the Netherlands has in the past been partly attributed to the uncertainty over the legal status of strike action.[6] What effect this has had on the duration of stoppages that do occur is questionable, however, but it does seem to have been partly effective in shortening the average length of stoppages, possibly after the instigation of legal action to terminate a strike.

United Kingdom

The UK produces a comprehensive list of duration categories and these have been condensed into three broad groupings in Table 14.6.[7] The application of a minimum size threshold will tend to discount some of the smallest disputes, though it is a less restrictive minimum than is used in some of the other countries, e.g. Ireland and Denmark.

Table 14.6 Duration of stoppages in the UK (annual average percentage 1972–81, stoppages beginning in each year)

	Stoppages	Working days lost
Less than 2 days	31.5	3.0
2–5 days	25.2	5.6
5 days and over	43.3	91.4
All	100.0	100.0

Source: Employment Gazette, Department of Employment.

The figures show that approximately 31.5 per cent of all recorded stoppages lasted less than two working days yet these accounted for only 3 per cent of all working time lost. As in the other countries covered so far, the majority of working days lost are accounted for by a disproportionate number of larger stoppages. Overall, though, many stoppages of work will go unrecorded because they will fall below the minimum size for inclusion.

The USA

The fifth country to publish regular statistics on the duration of stoppages is the USA, and again prior to 1982 there was an extensive listing of duration categories. This permits the compilation of the statistics in Table 14.7 which draws on the ten-year period 1972–81 and shows both stoppages and working days lost.

The US minimum size qualification for inclusion until the end of 1981 (stoppages must last at least one full day and involve at least six workers) is less restrictive than some others, but will inevitably exclude some of the smallest stoppages. The figures in Table 14.7 show that over the ten-year period the average number

Table 14.7 Duration of stoppages in the USA (annual average percentages 1972–81, stoppages ending in each year)

	Stoppages	Working days lost
1 day	13.6	0.5
2–6 days	22.3	3.2
7–29 days	34.6	18.5
30 days and over	29.5	77.8
All	100.0	100.0

Source: Analysis of Work Stoppages, Bureau of Labor Statistics.

of stoppages lasting for one day amounted to 13.6 per cent of the total, but only 0.5 per cent of all working time lost. Compared to the other two countries which have a broadly similar higher category of duration as shown in the foregoing tables, namely Belgium and Ireland (actually thirty-one days and over compared to the USA thirty days and over), it is clear that the duration of stoppages in the USA is appreciably greater. In Belgium only 6.2 per cent of all stoppages lasted longer than thirty-one days, while in Ireland the corresponding figure was 12.2 per cent, but in the USA it was much higher at 29.5 per cent.

Other comparisons of duration data between countries is difficult, given the use of different bands of duration. However, what is clear from the statistics of the five countries presented above is that there is a common pattern with a high proportion of total stoppages accounting for a much smaller proportion of total working time lost as a result. This, above all else, underlines the use of working days lost as the best measure of stoppage activity to use in any international comparisons, since it will be less affected as an overall measure by the use of minimum size criteria, but also the inevitable non-recording (no matter what the system of measurement is) of the smallest disputes.

The trend in duration

It is interesting to pursue the trends in the duration of recorded stoppages in each country and in particular to look at the possible effects of economic recession on the patterns of duration, assuming that there is such a perceptible pattern.

The effects of a depressed economy and poor labour market conditions on the duration of stoppages can be seen from two conflicting aspects. The first sees the effects of recession as having a moderating influence on the workers' decision both to take strike action and to prolong the period of the strike once into it. This should, therefore, have the effect of reducing the average length of stoppages that are called.

This viewpoint is counteracted to some extent by the likely reactions of management in industries affected by recession. In good times, it is likely that employers will want to find solutions to strikes that are called as quickly as possible in order to restore normal production and hence maintain sales of the product or service. However, in times of recession, with depressed sales, the impetus for resolving disputes quickly is less strong and so there should be a tendency for disputes on average to last longer.

In reality, the actual effect of changes in economic fortunes is likely to be a combination of both factors, each of which tends to pull against the other with a resultant small net effect.

The available statistics on duration in the five countries that actually publish details can have only a limited use in determining such effects. Recent information (that is for 1980 and 1981) is only available in three of the five countries—Ireland, the UK and the USA—and so these have been used to illustrate the trends over the period 1977–81, which covers the current economic recession which is generally thought to have started in all three countries around 1979–80. Table 14.8 summarises the results.

Table 14.8 Trend in stoppages by duration

		1977	1978	1979	1980	1981
Ireland*						
	1–10 days	65.1	66.5	62.8	60.0	59.0
	11 days and over	34.9	33.5	37.2	40.0	41.0
UK*						
	2–5 days	57.4	59.0	56.7	65.6	68.2
	5 days and over	42.6	41.0	43.3	34.4	31.8
USA†						
	1–6 days	34.3	28.1	29.4	25.8	25.4
	7 days and over	65.7	71.9	70.6	74.2	74.6

*Stoppages beginning in each year.   † Stoppages ending in each year.
Source: National statistics.

In the case of two of the three countries, Ireland and the USA, there is no significant change in the proportion of recorded stoppages between the lower and upper duration bands, as illustrated in Table 14.8. In both countries the broad bands of duration used differ, but the only discernible trend is a general movement of the figures towards greater proportions in the longer duration categories, but this has been more or less continuous over the five-year period.

In the UK, however, there does appear to be a discernible shift in the proportions around 1979–80, such that whereas in 1979 the number of stoppages lasting for five days and over accounted for 43.3 per cent of the total, this had decreased to 34.4 per cent in 1980 and to 31.8 per cent the following year. This could be taken to indicate that in the UK, at least, the effect of the most recent economic recession has been to shorten the duration of some disputes.

Cause and duration

Earlier in the chapter, the possible relationship between the cause of a stoppage and its duration was mentioned. Since then it has been demonstrated that on average in most countries, the majority of all stoppages are caused by issues concerned with wages and other essentially financial issues and so it will inevitably be the case that most time lost will be due to this cause. Unfortunately, the almost total absence of readily available data which can show the relationship between cause and duration prohibits extensive comparisons between countries. In fact the only country to produce such a cross-classification of the data is the USA and since the changeover to a more restricted definition in January 1982, data are only available up to the end of 1981.

The classification by cause is relatively well detailed and all the usual categories are listed in Table 14.9. The four bands of duration also shown in the table have been aggregated from the usual eight in the interests of simplicity. The figures are for 1980 only and so should not be taken as absolute guides to other years, though examination of previous years reveals that the same kind of causes arise in similar proportions. For example, in 1980 the proportion of all disputes attributed to wage issues in the USA was 70.8 per cent (in Table 14.9 it is the aggregate of the first three categories: general wage changes, supplementary benefits and wage adjustments). Comparing this to the annual average figure for the period 1972–81 in Table 14.1 shows this to be not significantly different at 67.6 per cent.

Table 14.9 Duration of stoppages by cause in the USA (percentage of working days lost 1980)

	1 day	2–6 days	7–29 days	30 days and over	Total	Percentage of all causes
General wage changes	0.1	2.5	17.9	79.5	100.0	65.9
Supplementary benefits	0.4	3.3	24.9	71.4	100.0	0.7
Wage adjustments	0.1	0.7	1.6	97.6	100.0	4.2
Hours of work	–	5.7	24.3	70.0	100.0	–
Other contractual matters	0.5	1.4	19.1	79.0	100.0	2.2
Union organisation and security	0.1	3.8	28.8	67.3	100.0	2.4
Job security	0.2	1.2	38.5	60.1	100.0	9.8
Plant administration	0.6	3.5	2.9	93.0	100.0	14.2
Other working conditions	2.3	20.4	7.3	70.0	100.0	0.3
Inter- or intra-union matters	6.7	22.5	69.4	1.4	100.0	0.2
Not reported	1.7	11.8	44.5	42.0	100.0	0.1
All causes	0.2	2.5	17.5	79.8	100.0	100.0

Source: *Analysis of Work Stoppages*, US Bureau of Labor Statistics.

The figures in Table 14.9 show that in the USA for 1980, for most of the causes listed, the majority of working days lost were due to the longer duration disputes. The only exception to this rule might be the case of stoppages caused by inter-union or intra-union matters. Here the majority of working days lost were in the duration band 7–29 days with a figure of 69.4 per cent. There was only 1.4 per cent of all working days lost attributable to the longest duration category of 30 days and over. Could this mean that disputes between or within trade unions are resolved more quickly? Certainly this could be the case especially since in many such disputes the general involvement of management in the deliberations may speed the negotiation process up considerably.

Overall, the results of Table 14.9 show that, as would be expected, few days are lost in those stoppages of short duration, no matter what the cause is, further confirming the generalised pattern of activity displayed in other measures and classifications already discussed. Of course this relates just to one country's experience and only during one year which may not be typical of either other countries or other periods. However, in the absence of the relevant statistics in the other countries there is no way of checking this out.

Notes

1. In the case of Germany, for example, where union strike benefits are considered to be high in comparison with other countries, they probably do not exceed 55 to 75 per cent of normal earnings. See Kennedy, T., *European Labor Relations* (Lexington, D.C. Heath, 1980), p. 181.
2. McCarthy, W., 'The reasons given for striking: an analysis of official statistics 1945-57', *Bulletin of the Oxford Institute of Economics and Statistics,* Vol. 21 (1959). Reproduced in Evans, E. W. and Creigh, S. W. (eds), *Industrial Conflict in Britain* (London, Frank Cass, 1977), Chapter 7.
3. Batstone, E., Boraston, I. and Frenkel, S., *The Social Organisation of Strikes* (Oxford, Basil Blackwell, 1978).
4. Hyman, R., *Strikes* (London, Collins/Fontana, 1972), pp. 19-24.
5. The duration bands used here are aggregates of the more detailed groupings regularly published by each country. The exact bands used can be found in each relevant national chapter in Part II.
6. Discussed in Kennedy, T., op. cit., p. 125.
7. The duration categories were changed in 1979, such that the bands from 5 to 6 days onwards were different from those prior to 1979.

15   STRIKE-PRONENESS IN INDUSTRIES

There has already been much discussion of the differences in stoppage activity amongst industries and this chapter carries the discussion further, bringing in the somewhat limited possibilities for international comparisons. However, in concentrating on differences in industries, it should not be forgotten that differences in strike-proneness can be evidenced in other factors such as location, and more importantly, occupations, though the latter factor in particular suffers from a poor supply of information in all of the nine countries covered here, which prohibits any useful comparisons.[1] In addition, the broader comparisons of national disputes activity have already been covered in Chapter 13.

Before launching into a discussion of the strike-proneness of different industries it is important to put the overall extent of such activity into perspective. From work done in the UK, it is possible to get some idea of the proportion of firms experiencing some kind of industrial action. For example, Smith *et al.,* in their analysis of stoppages over the period 1968–73, found that in an average year only around 2 per cent of all manufacturing establishments, employing around 20 per cent of the total labour force in that particular sector, experienced a stoppage.[2] This means that the vast majority of plants were unaffected by any stoppages whatsoever.

Similarly, the manufacturing sector was the subject of a special workplace survey held in 1977/78 in Great Britain. The results of the survey, published in Brown, show in more detail the experience of strike action over a two-year period.[3] For example, it was found that approximately 46 per cent of establishments in the survey reported an incidence of industrial action by manual workers, but only 9 per cent for non-manual workers. For strikes alone the corresponding proportions were approximately one-third for manual workers and only about 5 per cent for non-manuals.

All the evidence, therefore, points to the observation that the majority of manufacturing establishments are unaffected by stoppages. Though the information presented above specifically relates to the UK, it would be fair to assume that it would also be applicable to the other eight countries in this study, given the relatively high recorded level of stoppage activity in the UK and the extent of the manufacturing sector (explained in more detail below) in all the countries. However, this generalisation will mask the concentration of stoppage activity in those sectors within manufacturing which are particularly strike-prone, so due consideration needs to be given to this point also.

Industries affected

There has been some previous coverage of the nature of strike-prone industries in each of the nine countries. The UK in particular has been covered well in such works as those of Shorey[4] or Edwards[5] which have explored the determinants of strike-proneness and which undoubtedly have wider implications beyond just the UK. In France the epic, but now dated, work by Shorter and Tilly covers a long period of strike activity in that country.[6] Unfortunately, few works have approached the problem of international comparisons.

One exception is the comparative work of Kerr and Siegel, which examined the statistics in eleven countries, of which Germany, Italy, the Netherlands, the UK and the USA are common to this study.[7] But again the work is now quite dated. However, using the aggregated data on working days lost and labour force size, the authors determined that the propensity to strike was highest in mining and the maritime and longshore (dock workers, for example) sectors. The lowest propensities were found to be in the railways, agriculture and trade (distributive) industries. Whether or not these sectors are still holding their league positions is difficult to say. Certainly in those countries where such sectors are particularly prominent (for example mining in the UK and the USA, or agriculture in France and Ireland) it would seem that these are still displaying high and low strike propensities respectively (see the relevant tables in the national chapters in Part II).

Determinants of strike-proneness

The reasons why different industries are more strike-prone than others are various. Foremost amongst these will be the basic structure of the industry in terms of size of establishment and nature of the production process, but in addition other factors such as location, the relative position of the industry (in the sense that are the workers in a strong position to exercise much industrial 'muscle'?) and the past history of such action will all have an important effect.

Shorey found that there are three key internal factors which will have a strong influence on strike activity within an individual industry or plant.[8] These are the proportion of females in the total workforce, the relative importance of payment-by-results systems, and the size of the establishment. The latter factor has been explored in great detail in the literature, and most of the work tends to point to the positive effect it has on strike frequency.[9] Thus it is not surprising to find that those industries characterized by large-size plants, e.g. motor vehicles production, will tend to appear strike-prone in comparison to most other sectors.

Of course, the concept of strike-proneness is relative. It will be a reflection of the overall disputes activity within each country, which may mean that it is unreasonable to compare such activity across countries. If one country has an exceptionally low overall level of disputes activity, then this is likely to lead to low levels of activity in most industry groups, though there will still be prominent sectors.

To summarise, the determination of the relative strike-proneness of a particular industry will be a function of a complex set of factors, the combination of which will inevitably lead to those industries experiencing higher than average levels of strike activity.

Employment by broad sector

It is clear, therefore, that the incidence of stoppages will be strongly linked to the relative importance of certain sectors in each country. In the nine countries examined here there are differences in the proportions of the total workforce in the four broad sectors of primary, manufacturing, construction and services, as shown in Table 15.1, covering 1980. These differences in the structure of employment must undoubtedly contribute to the variations in stoppage activity when the statistics are compared internationally. The statistics show that in the primary sector, seven of the nine countries have only a small proportion of the total labour force employed in this sector, mainly in agriculture and mining. The two exceptions are Ireland and Italy where the primary sector accounts for 20.2 and 15.3 per cent respectively of the total employed labour force. In the manufacturing sector, Germany has the greatest proportion at 35.1 per cent and the Netherlands and Denmark have the smallest at 21.3 per cent each. The construction industry takes up to 10 per cent of the employed labour force in the case of Italy, and this is slightly above most of the other countries. The nine country average is 8.2 per cent.

Table 15.1 Civilian employment by industrial sector (percentage of total employment in each sector, 1980)

	Primary	Manufacturing	Construction	Services	All industries and services
Belgium	3.8	25.4	7.7	63.1	100.0
Denmark*	8.3	21.3	8.0	62.4	100.0
France	9.5	25.7	8.6	56.2	100.0
Germany	7.3	35.1	7.6	50.0	100.0
Ireland	20.2	21.2	8.9	49.7	100.0
Italy	15.3	26.7	10.0	48.0	100.0
Netherlands	6.0	21.3	9.5	63.2	100.0
UK	4.1	28.4	6.9	60.6	100.0
USA	4.5	22.1	6.3	67.1	100.0
9-country average	8.8	25.2	8.2	57.8	100.0

*1979 figures.
Source: *Labour Force Statistics*, OECD.

This leaves the services sector to account for the major differences in the relative proportions of employment. The nine country average is 57.8 per cent, but this is exceeded by five countries, with the highest percentage in the USA with 67.1 per cent. Those countries with the largest employment in the primary sector, Ireland and Italy, show the smallest proportions in services at 49.7 and 48 per cent respectively.

Comparison of broad sectors

All nine countries publish regular details of stoppages by industry groups, in fact it is the only classification of the data regularly produced by all countries. The problem is, however, that each country uses its own breakdown of industrial activities which inhibits detailed comparisons by industry across the countries.

The best that can be done is to group each industry into the four broad sectors of primary, manufacturing, construction and services, the latter to include public utilities (such as gas and electricity supply industries) and transport services. The individual national tables of working days lost by industry are given in the national chapters in Part II. Here Table 15.2 presents the annual average figures for the period 1972–81 (where the statistics permit), showing the number of working days lost per 1,000 workers in that particular sector for each of the nine countries.

In all the nine countries except the USA, working days lost per 1,000 workers were highest in the manufacturing sector, though with considerable variation in the overall figures. For example, Germany had the lowest average with only 47 days lost per 1,000 workers, with the Netherlands not far behind with 81 days lost. Most of the other countries were showing much larger figures topped by Italy with 1,825 days lost and the UK with 1,073.

Table 15.2 Working days lost per 1,000 workers by broad industry group (annual averages 1972–81)

	Primary	Manufacturing	Construction	Services	All industries and services
Belgium*	1	576	5	10	173
Denmark†	**	690	436	64	241
France‡	191	323	83	81	156
Germany‡	2	47	5	5	29
Ireland‡	156	745	362	563	496
Italy §	437	1,825	664	564	870
Netherlands‡	**	81	12	15	30
UK‡	752	1,073	438	174	493
USA‡	891	711	912	166	371

*Annual average for 1972–80 only.
†Figures for 1980 and 1981 use 1979 labour force size.
‡Figures for 1981 use 1980 labour force size
§ Annual average for 1972–80 only. Figures for 1972–77 use 1977 labour force size.
**Under one working day lost per 1,000 workers
Source: National statistics, *Labour Force Statistics,* OECD

In Belgium, Denmark, Germany and the Netherlands, the average number of days lost in the primary sector was extremely low, the highest being in Germany but then with only two days lost per 1,000 workers. This is despite a large coal-mining industry in that country, which, elsewhere, has been noted for its relatively high levels of disputes activity.[10] The other two countries with large coal-mining sectors, the UK and the USA, show significantly large numbers of working days lost per 1,000 workers in the primary sector, being 752 and 891 respectively. In the case of the UK, over the ten-year period, mining and quarrying (but mainly coal-mining) accounted for 99.8 per cent of all days lost in the primary sector (see Table 11.4). In the USA the corresponding figure for mining was 95.5 per cent (see Table 12.3).

In most of the nine countries, the construction industry had a fairly high level of days lost per 1,000 workers (in construction), with that sector in the USA showing the highest figure of the four countries, with 912 days lost per 1,000 workers. The exceptions to the majority were Belgium, Germany and the Netherlands, all with particularly low recorded figures.

The fourth sector—services—has had a comparatively favourable record of stoppage activity in all nine countries, despite the fact that the group includes transport workers, for example, who have had a tendency towards higher than average levels of strike action in most of the countries. The exceptions in this broad sector are Ireland and Italy, where the number of working days lost per 1,000 workers in the sector are 563 and 564 respectively. The nearest countries to these two is the UK, but well below their levels with only 174 days lost.

Overall, the statistics in Table 15.2 show that the distribution of working days lost over the four broad sectors of industrial activity is uneven, even when expressed in terms of the number of workers in each sector. As would be expected, those countries with low overall levels of strike activity such as Germany and the Netherlands, have similarly low rates of activity in each sector. Clearly, though, in all countries the services have the best record overall, but then this is very much a reflection of the structure of that sector in terms of smaller business units, for example.

Unfortunately the statistics presented for each country are still affected by differences in the definitions applied to the data collected. In France, for example, the sectors of agriculture and public administration are excluded from the statistics, so those broad sectors containing these groups would be affected accordingly. In Denmark there are significant problems with the statistics because of the method of collection of the basic information. This is done through the employers' federations and will inevitably exclude any non-members of such federations, with further problems of coverage caused by the casual method of collection. Therefore, as with all cases of international comparisons of strike activity, the industry data should be treated with caution.

Notes

1. There has been some comparative work on occupations in the UK where the availability of data is better than in most of the other countries. See, for example, Creigh, S. and Makeham, P., 'Strikers occupations: an analysis', *Employment Gazette* (March 1980), pp. 237-9, which uses unpublished data for the period 1966-73.
2. Smith, C. T. B., Clifton, R., Makeham, P., Creigh, S. W. and Burn, R. V.,

Strikes in Britain (London, DE Manpower Paper No. 15, HMSO, 1978), Chapter 8. Some of the results were first reported in an article, 'The distribution and concentration of industrial stoppages in Great Britain', *Employment Gazette* (November 1976), pp. 1219-24.

3. Brown, W. (ed.), *The Changing Contours of British Industrial Relations* (Oxford, Basil Blackwell, 1981), see especially Chapter 5.
4. Shorey, J., 'An inter-industry analysis of strike frequency', *Economica*, Vol. 43:4 (1976), pp. 349-65.
5. Edwards, P. K., 'The strike-proneness of British manufacturing establishments', *British Journal of Industrial Relations*, Vol. 19:2 (1981), pp. 135-48.
6. Shorter, E. and Tilly, C., *Strikes in France 1830-1968* (Cambridge, Cambridge University Press, 1974).
7. Kerr, C. and Siegel, A., 'The inter-industry propensity to strike—an international comparison'. Originally published in Kornhauser, A., Dubin, R. and Ross, A. M., *Industrial Conflict* (New York, McGraw-Hill, 1954). Reprinted in Evans, E. W. and Creigh, S. W., *Industrial Conflict in Britain* (London, Frank Cass, 1977), Chapter 11.
8. Shorey, J., op. cit.
9. See for example, Edwards, P. K., 'Size of plant and strike-proneness', *Oxford Bulletin of Economics and Statistics*, Vol. 42:2 (1980), pp. 145-56. Also Churnside, R. J. and Creigh, S. W., 'Strike activity and plant size: a note', *Journal of the Royal Statistical Society*, Vol. 144:1 (1981), pp. 104-11.
10. In Rimlinger, G. V., 'International differences in the strike propensity of coal miners: experience in four countries', *Industrial and Labor Relations Review*, Vol. 12:3 (1959), reprinted in Evans, E. W. and Creigh, S. W., op. cit., it is stated that coal-miners in France, Germany, the UK and the USA have a lot in common with an 'inherent environmental tendency toward strike-proneness', but this tendency may be affected by 'socio-cultural' factors in each case. This, in part, could explain the relatively low strike record of German miners, for example, in comparison to their fellow miners in the other countries.

16 TRADE UNIONS AND INDUSTRIAL RELATIONS STRUCTURES

In this chapter the relative size and importance of trade unions and the machinery that exists for the conduct of industrial relations in each of the nine countries are discussed. Inevitably, however, given the limits of space available and the author's own ability in this complex subject area, the discussion will be brief and will mainly aim to provide an outline of the situation in each country, drawing comparisons where appropriate. Of course, implicit in this discussion is the assumption that both trade unions and systems of industrial relations have some influence on the incidence of stoppages of work, and also help to shape their form when they do occur, measured in terms of such factors as their duration and distribution by industry and occupation.

Much has been written on the potential influence of trade unions on the incidence of stoppages, but most of this has been focused at a national level as, for example, in the case of Clegg for the UK.[1] Nevertheless such studies provide lessons beyond those for the individual country under scrutiny. However, there have been a few studies which have looked at the differences in trade unions and industrial relations structures across countries as a possible explanation of different strike propensities. It is also possible from the paucity of statistics available in some of the nine countries covered in this study to assess the likely extent of union involvement in all stoppage activity.

Goodman attributes many of the differences in national trade union and collective bargaining structures to historical factors and to their development out of established national institutions, in many cases being derivatives of them.[2] This can go a long way to explain the significant differences that do exist between countries but there still remains the question of the real effect that both factors have on the incidence of strikes. The basic argument is that trade unions, because of their fundamental (and simplified) aim of improving the lot of their members, will tend to be involved in any call for strike action since the only way for such action to be effective is to have significant collective support, and this requires a high degree of organisation. Furthermore, to some extent the propensity and ultimately the efficacy of this action will be strongly influenced by the facilities that exist for either preventing disputes developing into stoppages of work in the first place (for example, through conciliation and arbitration facilities) but ultimately for resolving them once they have occurred.

Trade union involvement

The extent of trade union involvement in stoppages of work can be simply tested by examining the proportion of stoppages classified as 'official', that is those with union recognition at an executive committee level (see Chapter 2). This is perhaps a naive view of union involvement since in many so-called 'unofficial' disputes there will be a considerable degree of involvement, usually of shop-floor representatives, in many of them. Batstone *et al.* have emphasised that for strikes to happen and to be effective in terms of worker support, there must be sufficient organisation and this usually comes through the recognised focus for grievances, the shop steward.[3]

Of the nine countries studied here only one, the UK, actually publishes separate details of the stoppages classified as unofficial. The extent of such action over the period 1971–80 has already been documented in Table 2.1. This shows that of all stoppages during the ten-year period, only 4.7 per cent were classified as official, which accounted for 42.4 per cent of all workers involved and 61 per cent of all working days lost. Of course the number of stoppages measured in the UK will be affected by the non-recording of the smallest disputes, with these falling under the minimum size threshold for inclusion. But, since most of these smaller stoppages will be spontaneous (wildcat) stoppages which have not had time to become formalised, they cannot be considered as possible official disputes. Therefore, it is clear that the majority of stoppages in the UK are unofficial, but generally account for few working days lost as a proportion of the total.

However, according to Clegg, a further complication arises in the UK (though it may also have wider applicability in other countries) in distinguishing unofficial stoppages because some start unofficially but are given union recognition once they have got underway.[4] Others, it is pointed out, are given what is called 'quasi-approval' by the union in the form of a financial grant in lieu of strike pay. In such cases the union still maintains a low profile during the dispute but inevitably exercises considerable control over it.

The incidence of official compared to unofficial stoppages in other countries is difficult to assess in the absence of separate statistics. However, the limited evidence available suggests that there may be great variations in each country. For example, in the USA Clegg has estimated, on the basis that those strikes which occur at the end of a collective agreement are considered both constitutional and therefore lawful, that about two-thirds of all stoppages recorded can be considered as official. Unfortunately, the only other country where it is reasonably safe to assess the official and unofficial mix is Germany. In that country there are strict conditions embodied in the labour law that for a strike to be legal it must have the authorisation of the relevant trade union. In addition, the DGB, the trade union confederation, imposes its own strict conditions on affiliated unions initiating strikes. Taking all this into account and given the comparatively small number of stoppages anyway in Germany, the vast majority of them must be considered official.

Therefore, it would appear that the determinants of the extent of union involvement in stoppages will be a function of a complex set of factors which may be only relevant to individual countries. In particular it will involve consideration of the organisation and extent of trade unions and, more importantly, the conditions that exist in the labour law of each country and how this affects the recognition of industrial action generally.

Trade union membership

The paucity of data available on the membership of trade unions in all nine countries prevents extensive comparisons of the effects of unions on disputes activity. In particular there are no reliable statistics on the extent of female membership, for example, which could be an important factor to take into account, but then traditionally unionisation amongst women has been relatively low in all countries. More important is the poor data on the density of membership by industry and the extent of multi-union plants.

Basic information about membership in the nine countries is given in Table 16.1. The information in most cases is fairly recent (1981) but nevertheless should be treated with caution. The most important qualification is that methods of measurement vary between countries and in some the figures are no more than simple estimates based on a composite of information sources. In Italy, for example, though the figures show that there are around seven million trade union members in the country, Kennedy points out that in many cases those paying the requisite union dues are much fewer than this figure.[6] In one large plant it was found that only

Table 16.1 Trade union membership (figures for 1981 unless otherwise stated)

	Membership (000)	Density %
Belgium	2,641	75.0
Denmark*	1,588	70.5
France	5,550	22.7
Germany*	9,400	40.5
Ireland†	671	65.0
Italy	7,148	43.0
Netherlands	1,459	30.0
UK	12,250	51.0
USA‡	22,463	25.9

*Figures for 1980.
†Figures for 1978.
‡Figures for 1976.
Source: European Trade Union Institute; Eurostat Social Indicators; US Bureau of Labor Statistics.

14 per cent had their dues stopped from their pay. Therefore, actual active membership (if the payment of dues is considered a proxy for active membership) may be considerably smaller.

The statistics in Table 16.1 show that union membership density (that is membership as a percentage of labour force) is highest in Belgium with approximately 75 per cent of all workers belonging to a union.[7] Belgium is followed by Denmark with 70.5 per cent and Ireland with 65 per cent. There are then three countries with between 40.5 and 51 per cent membership—Germany, Italy and the UK—before the remaining three countries of the Netherlands, the USA and France come in with around one quarter of their labour forces unionised, the lowest being France with 22.7 per cent.

Expressed in these simple figures, there is considerable variation in the extent of trade union membership amongst the nine countries, but what the figures fail to show are the levels of membership in different industries and different occupations. In general, there is a higher level of unionisation in manual rather than non-manual jobs, though the trend is changing with a significant move in most of the countries to blue and white-collar unions.

In terms of the industrial distribution of membership, in most of the countries the concentration levels vary considerably. This to some extent will depend on the treatment of the closed shop in each nation, which arguably is the single most important determinant of union density in some industries.

The closed shop is described by Hanson, Jackson and Miller as the main method adopted by unions to attain 'security'.[8] Security in this sense means maximum union membership ideally achieved with no dissenters within an industry or plant. However, in many countries such efforts at security are seen as unlawful, and such restrictive practices are frequently outlawed. For example, in the UK the closed shop in all its forms is generally allowed, though there is the likelihood that its operation will be curtailed by proposed legislation in the near future. At the other extreme, in Italy and France any form of closed shop is considered illegal and is, therefore, banned.

Somewhere between these extremes lie the cases of the USA and Germany, for example, where in the former country the condition that an employee must join a union before being employed, or the pre-entry closed shop, is illegal under US law, but post-entry conditions are allowed.[9] In Germany, the law may be interpreted that employees have the right either to choose to enter a union or not, which by implication would make a pre-entry closed shop illegal.

Hanson *et al.* argue that there are certain types of occupations which lend themselves easily to the closed shop irrespective of the legality of it.[10] These 'closed shop prone' workers include craftsmen, certain types of casual labour (for example dock workers), those in community-based labour (for example coal-mining) and the professions. All these groups will have a natural tendency to group together and establish their own secure entry conditions. In view of this fact, the industrial structure of a country, with respect to these types of occupation, will have a strong influence on the pressure for closed shop practices.

Trade union structures

The structure of the trade union movement within each country will be a critical factor in determining the influence of the movement on the nature and pattern of strikes. By structure is meant the type of union, and usually three main types are distinguished though there are additional, but less important, ones. The three main types are: industrial, craft and general unions. Industrial unions cover a variety of different occupations within one industry (for example in coal-mining or motor car manufacturing) though they tend to be restricted to manual or non-manual employees in the industry. Craft unions, as the name implies, cover a specific skill or trade and may cut across a number of different industries, but equally employers may be faced with dealing with a number of different craft unions within the same establishment. Finally, general unions cover almost anyone who wants to join regardless of industry and occupation, and naturally these tend to be both broad in their coverage and large in size.

To the three main categories could be added a fourth, the professional bodies such as those which cover say medicine or accountancy in most of the nine countries covered here. Though strictly speaking they are not classified as trade unions, their method of operation in terms of looking after members' interests and being perhaps the chief exponents of the closed shop (achieved through their strict entrance qualifications) makes them all but, except in name only.[11] However, on the available evidence in the nine countries it does appear that their propensity to strike is exceptionally low compared to the more traditionally regarded craft unions.

The possible effects that trade union structures have on the propensity to strike are relatively straightforward, from a theoretical point of view. It is argued that from the employers' point of view, it is easier to deal with just one union covering the whole establishment labour force than with a multiplicity of unions. Clearly this latter situation will only be achieved with an industrial union. The employer can then avoid many of the problems that arise from inter-union disputes, commonly demarcation or jurisdictional disputes mostly found in those establishments with a number of different craft unions, but also arising where there is more than one type of any union.

As far as the nine countries are concerned, there is considerable variation in the types of unions that exist. These differences have been greatly influenced by historical developments which have shaped both the type of union and the attitudes towards them from government, employer and employee. A significant factor in many cases has been the degree of political attachment the union movement has had. For example, most of the nine countries have trade union movements that can be easily identified with a political party, in particular the identification taking the form of both similarities in aims and aspirations, but also in the unions providing financial support for their political affiliates. Out of the nine countries, probably the weakest union movement in terms of political power is that in the USA, but then even here it seems that, persuaded to a decision on their political stance, most unions would associate with the Democrats and most members would probably vote the same way.

The simplest structure is by far that found in Germany, but in many ways it is this way because of an historical accident. In that country there are only sixteen large industrial unions (though in fact the industries are broadly defined to include many subgroups who may only have a limited relationship with the named industry). They arose after the Second World War, following the break-up of the other older union structure, which had been based on political and religious affiliations. In other words, they were started from scratch and thus avoided many, if not all, of the problems that now afflict the union movements in the other countries mainly because of their long and fragmented stages of development.

For the other countries, they can be identified into clear groups with common union structures in the broadest sense. Certainly the 'Continental' countries are still characterised by the confederation of individual unions along either political or religious lines, as was the case in Germany before the Second World War. In the Netherlands, for example, there are approximately thirty-nine individual unions organised into three confederations, one socialist (and the largest), one catholic and the third non-denominational. In France there are five such confederations and four in Italy (though all political). In all three countries there are virtually no craft or general unions, but rather industrial unions.

The second group of countries would include the UK and Ireland, where the development of unions in both countries has been much the same and in many ways interdependent. Here there is the mix of all three types of union, with the industrial union being perhaps the least conspicuous. In the UK there are about 460 independent unions and fewer than 100 in Ireland, and most employers are faced with the problems posed by multi-unionism. The jurisdictional strike has been a familiar problem in both countries despite, for example, the efforts of the TUC in Britain to provide facilities through its 'Bridlington' procedure for resolving inter-union disputes.[12] The overall trend, however, has been towards amalgamation, with many of the smaller unions being swallowed up by the large general unions.

The third type identified amongst the nine countries includes only one country, the USA. Here there are about 170 unions (in 1978), mainly industrial but with a few craft. Most of the industrial unions are large in membership terms, though overall the density of union membership is comparatively low nationally (as shown in Table 16.1). It has already been pointed out that whereas most of the European unions can claim some political affiliation, the USA movement is less inclined to do so. In addition, the unions are strongest at a local plant level where most of the bargaining takes place, which may have the effect of dissipating solidarity at an executive level. Certainly a significant factor in dampening national union solidarity must be the geographical size of the country, with the inherent divergences of views and difficulties in communication.

In all nine countries most of the individual unions are arranged into confederations, which both co-ordinate activities and attempt to act as one voice on many matters. In Germany, Ireland, the UK and the USA, there is one predominant confederation, though affiliation levels vary considerably. For example, in the UK the TUC has almost 90 per cent of all trade union membership affiliated to it, while in the USA the much weaker AFL-CIO equivalent can claim only about 50 per cent of total membership. The highest level of affiliation is in Germany, where all the big sixteen industrial unions belong to the DGB, which has a considerable degree of influence over member unions. To these four countries could be added Denmark, where the national confederation, the Landsorganisationen (LO) has the majority of individual unions affiliated to it. However, in Denmark there is considerable emphasis on the local branch union and its role as part of its national organisation.

For the remaining four countries of Belgium, France, Italy and the Netherlands, the grouping of individual trade unions is dominated by a few confederations, each with their own political and/or religious backgrounds. Each of the national confederations will tend to be represented within an establishment so that in the case of a plant employing machine operators, for example, the employer will usually be faced with dealing with two or more confederations each representing their own member machine operators. But in most of these countries, the more contentious issues are dealt with on a broader plain than at plant level, and so many of the issues that emerge will relate to comparatively minor problems.

One significant factor which has developed over recent years has been the inevitable decline in the membership of trade unions as a result of rising unemployment. In most of the countries under study, unemployed union members who do not pay their dues are considered to be inactive members of the union and should, therefore, not be counted. Apart from the case of Denmark, where unions are still strongly involved with the payment of unemployment benefits, the majority of unions will have little to offer an unemployed member and so there will be little incentive for the member to continue paying dues. The decline in membership is significant because it inevitably weakens the power of the trade unions and their respective confederation. The decline has effect not only in terms of membership, but also in the related financial resources of the union through the loss of dues. Thus in recession there will be the combined effect of falling membership (and income) and a lower propensity to strike by workers, all of which will contribute to relatively low levels of activity.

Industrial relations

Trade unions will essentially operate within the existing framework for resolving disputes between management and worker found in each country. It is important, therefore, to consider the comparative industrial relations scene in each country with a view to helping explain the pattern and extent of stoppage activity. However, it should not be automatically assumed that mention of industrial relations in this context means only the mechanics of resolving disputes. In certain circumstances the existence of such factors as worker representation on the boards of companies or established consultation procedures, can go a long way to ensuring better industrial relations in the first place; a clear application of the 'prevention is better than cure' hypothesis.

But in most cases, the industrial relations scene in each country will be largely determined by the way disputes between worker or union and management are resolved. This will depend on the type and operation of the various mechanisms that exist for dealing with labour disputes, in particular the existence of institutions and labour law. Much of these, however, have grown up through time with additions and changes here and there which have usually resulted in a variety of institutions and legislation complicating any comparative assessment.

Clegg asserts that 'the pattern of strikes is . . . closely associated with the structure of bargaining in each country'.[13] This being so, it is essential to discuss the usual methods of collective bargaining used, especially for the main issues such as pay, holidays and the like. In particular, the type and level of bargaining will be important factors and, in addition, how any agreements reached actually affect the status of strikes, with such questions as are strikes during the currency of a collective agreement legal?

Because of the great diversity in the industrial relations structures in each of the nine countries, they will be tackled individually below. The summaries can only provide the broadest outline of what are essentially complex laws and institutional frameworks, but the intention is to give a flavour of the systems as opposed to any definitive product. In all this, it is fundamental to remember that the industrial relations structures are being examined for their possible influence on strike propensity and this underlines the rationale for any international comparisons.

Belgium

Collective bargaining in Belgium is usually carried out at three levels: the firm, the industrial sector and at a national level. However, it is at the national level that most of the major decisions are made and usually between the national components of the major employers' organisation, the Union of Belgian Enterprises (the VBO), and one of the main trade union confederations, normally either the Confederation of Christian Trade Unions (CSC) or the Belgian General Federation of Labour (FGTB).

Most of the collective agreements reached in the larger industries are drawn up by special 'joint committees' set up by statutory powers (embodied in 1945 and 1968 legislation) to be directly involved with the formulation of such agreements. The joint committees also have responsibility to ensure that in the event of any disputes, these are resolved quickly ideally, before any industrial action is taken.

In addition to the industry-wide concern for conciliation, another key to industrial peace is seen as the works councils at the enterprise level. In all firms with at least 150 employees, a representative works council must be formed, which, through legislation enacted in 1973, has a right to the disclosure of certain pieces of company information, as well as a say in the future path taken by the management of the company. This emphasis on co-determination is thought to provide good grounds for conciliation on any points at issue. In fact, it does appear that the Belgian industrial relations system is heavily reliant on the incentive effect, i.e. if workers are in an informed position about the company then that should moderate their demands and, ultimately, their decisions to take any industrial action.

Denmark

In Denmark, most of the major bargaining issues, such as overall wage increases, holiday entitlements and redundancy provisions, are dealt with at a national level between the appropriate representative bodies. In the case of workers, it has already been mentioned that the majority of unions are affiliated to the Landsorganisationen (LO) which is a relatively strong negotiating body. On the employers' side, the main employers' organisation is the Dansk Arbejdsgiver-forening, a confederation of employers' associations with a long history (founded in 1896) specifically to match the grouping of the trade unions and their growing demands.

The union movement has a strong local base with specific areas of operation but coming under the ultimate control of the national executive. The individual member employers' associations of the confederation are also, to some extent, organised on a geographical basis, though it has been shown that the number of individual associations number approximately 180 compared to only 40 or so national unions.[14] The amount of negotiation on issues between individual unions and employers' associations is more low-key than that discussed at a confederation level, and mainly relates to internal wage matters and other industry-specific points. This would appear to leave little left to discuss at a local level and so only the more minor issues are dealt with by the local representatives.

In his detailed work on the Danish system of industrial relations written in the early 1950s, Galenson points out that industrial relations in Denmark are both stable and organised, and this would still appear to be the case thirty years on.[15] Much of this organisation is due to the existence of both a high degree of co-operation between management and unions, with plenty of consultation through long-established machinery, but also the legislation (some of it dating back to 1910) incorporating the Labour Court which can work to resolve issues that arise during the currency of collective agreements. Generally, collective agreements are negotiated on the basis that there will be industrial peace during their currency, though this may not always happen in practice.

The main legislative basis for resolving disputes is embodied in the agreement drawn up and approved in 1910 by the main employers' and employees' representative bodies known as the 'Standard Rules'. They were embodied into the law by a 1934 Act and have remained more or less intact since. They provide for situations where disputes arise involving collective agreements that do not contain their own provisions for the resolution of disputes, and can have binding powers in such cases.

France

In France, the trade union movement is the weakest of the nine countries, as measured by membership density. Nevertheless, the individual unions, but more importantly the five main union federations, all play an active part in the determination of a whole range of working conditions. To match the consolidation of the trade unions, the employers are mainly organised into regional and national

associations based on their respective industries, and most are affiliated to the central representative body, the Conseil National du
Patronat Française (CNPF). The CNPF itself is involved with the
formulation of some agreements. Most such agreements are concerned with the broader issues of, for example, unemployment
benefits, hours of work and pensions, with less emphasis on pay
bargaining.

Labour agreements reached between employer and employee
representatives have a particularly strong status in France. They
can be legally enforced by either side in the event of any infringe-
ment of the agreement. Furthermore, each collective agreement
that does not contain specific procedures for conciliation in the
event of a dispute, will be automatically subject to conciliation
by a government-appointed committee. However, as Kennedy
points out, the law on this point is not clear as to whether the
conciliation is required *before* strike action is taken or only *after*
it has started.[16] Presumably strike action, if taken, is a clear signal
that the agreement has broken down and can only be resolved
by conciliation, so the majority of such intervention will probably
come after a strike has started.

As in many of the other European countries, in France there is
considerable emphasis, backed up by legislation, on the employees'
right to company information. For example, in all firms with fifty
or more workers, a consultative *comité d'enterprise* or works council
must be set up and provided with information. However, the councils
are only consultative bodies and do not have any rights to participation in the decision-making process, thus falling behind such countries
as Belgium, for example, where the emphasis is on co-determination.

Germany

Of the nine countries covered in this study, Germany appears to have
the most comprehensive set of rules and facilities for averting stoppages of work. The industrial relations system uses a combination
of legislation, facilities for working out problems and worker participation to control the end result of industrial disputes, all of
which, if judged on the Federal Republic's record of stoppages,
seems to work to advantage.

Of course in many ways the country had the undoubted advantage
of having to restructure its industrial relations system after the
1939–45 War. Thus all of the important legislation pertaining to
the control of labour disputes is comparatively recent and as a result
relatively co-ordinated. Furthermore, the union structure is well
defined, with the sixteen large industrial unions all affiliated to

the DGB, the trade union confederation, thereby making negotiations comparatively straightforward. In Germany, all trade unions must be independent from any political or religious organisations and so this element of potential conflict is also removed.[17]

Collective bargaining is generally the norm on a few issues only, and then at a state level rather than on a national or local level. The bargaining usually takes place between the industry trade union and the representative employers' association (there are around 800 of these covering most sectors of industry), and bargains agreed to and signed by each party are legally binding. Furthermore, most have an explicit (or sometimes implicit) in-built no-strike (or no lockout) clause. Thus any stoppage of work during the currency of these agreements would usually be considered a breach of the agreement and, therefore, illegal.

Many of the issues that in other countries would be dealt with by bargaining between labour and management are covered by legislative measures in Germany. These include such matters as dismissal procedures, holidays, redundancies or special benefits such as maternity entitlements. It is at the formulation of the legislation stage that the trade union movement tends to have some effect, proving its power as a pressure group. The employers' associations also influence the decisions on these social matters, though perhaps with less effect. Wage rates are not dealt with using legislation, of course, but again there is a well established procedure where basic minimum rates are agreed in each industry, though across different plants there may be considerable wage drift since individual employers are free to pay above the minimum rates.

In the event of disputes over almost any aspect of employment, including those involving the labour legislation and collective agreements, the Federal Republic has the facilities to resolve disputes quickly. This is achieved through the use of a system of labour courts, established under a 1953 Act which set up 113 local courts with support, mainly for appeals, in a further 11 regional courts (one for each state) and, ultimately, a national court. The courts can hear disputes brought before it by individuals as well as unions or employers' groups and conciliation is usually tried first. If this fails to succeed, then the courts will make a binding judgement. According to figures reported in Kennedy, the use of the labour courts does appear to be high, with an estimated 387,000 cases brought before them in 1975.[18] Furthermore, it is interesting to note that certainly over recent years the number of complaints brought to the courts has increased, though with the highest numbers in times of recession.[19]

Ireland

The industrial relations system in the Irish Republic has developed from the UK system in many respects, though, as Pollock points out, it is nevertheless a 'quite separate and distinct system'.[20] Free collective bargaining over most issues is the normal method of approach, with the bargaining taking place between the trade unions and either the individual employer or, in some cases, representative employers' associations. However, of the two sides in the bargaining equation, it is clear that the trade union side has the advantage in terms of its influence and strength.

The limits to the power of the unions are embodied in a series of legislative measures starting with the 1946 Industrial Relations Act which, amongst its provisions, established a labour court. The court has a non-legal status, however, and is mainly concerned with issuing recommendations to the parties in dispute, or providing a conciliation service. Nevertheless, its field of operation is quite wide and in recent years its use has increased significantly, amplifying its role in Irish industrial relations.

However, it is the emergence of centralised bargaining over pay that has been seen as the significant step in avoiding much potential conflict. The system emerged in 1970 with the first National Pay Agreement and there have been a series of them since. The Agreements are reached through structured discussions between employers and unions and usually through the established Employer-Labour Conference, which has a membership of both those employers from private and public industry and representatives from the Irish Congress of Trade Unions (ICTU).

Further evidence of the effort to subdue potential conflict between employer and worker has come through 1977 legislation. This made provision for worker directors to be elected to the boards of state enterprises (such as electricity supply and peat development, for example) to the extent that one-third of the membership of each board would be elected worker representatives. In addition, there is further recognition of the need for better information flow between employer and employee, which underline the concern in Ireland over establishing better industrial relations.

Italy

The Italian industrial relations scene is characterised by the limited extent of formalised legislation and established institutions regulating collective bargaining. Collective bargaining is the normal way of reaching agreement on a variety of issues, but not only limited to wages and the conditions of work. Frequently they will involve the desire to press for wider social reforms, as evidenced in the number of short duration protest strikes comparatively common in Italy (see Chapter 9).

The main bargaining organisations on the trade union side are the four major confederations, each one representing a group of industrial unions. In addition to the four confederations there are a few independent unions, but overall membership of these is small. For the employers, there are three main associations. The largest, Confindustria, covers industry, with parallel organisations for commerce and agriculture (known as Conforcommercio and Confaricoltura respectively). A fourth association, Intersind, covers public sector enterprises. Bargaining between these representative bodies usually takes place at two levels, industry and plant, sometimes known as 'articulated' bargaining. The national agreements usually cover the establishment of minima in such things as wages, bonuses and hours of work. These minima are then used as the basis for plant negotiations which endeavour to increase on the basis already agreed.

All collective agreements are entered into with less vigour than those in say Germany, for example. Thus they are open to renegotiation and during their course strikes may take place, since in most cases agreements containing no-strike clauses would be uneforceable.

Most of the legal framework surrounding the conduct of industrial relations is embodied in the Italian Constitution (of 1948) and subsequent regulatory legislation, such as those Acts covering unemployment benefits and dismissals, for example. An Act passed in 1970 was particularly important in establishing the rights of employees and trade unions, known as the 'Statuto dei Diritti dei Lavoratori'. It does seem, however, that most of the recent legislation has been aimed at formalising the various conditions already won through collective bargaining, and in this sense the influence of both unions and employers' organisations in the shaping of legislation is exceptionally strong.[21]

In the event of disputes that cannot be reconciled through bargaining between the two sides, there is no compulsory move to mediation and nor is there an established separate official mediation service. Assistance is available, in the majority of cases, however, from the Ministry of Labour and Social Security (Ministero del Lavoro e della Previdenza Sociale), and in the nationalised sector from the controlling ministry for the public sector. It is difficult to say how effective the facilities for negotiation are, but given their voluntary nature and the fact that most strikes in Italy are of short duration anyway, it would seem that their overall effect on the level of stoppage activity is relatively small.

The Netherlands

In general, the industrial relations perspective in the Netherlands is one which is very much dependent on the agreement of issues through collective bargaining. However, the bargaining takes place within a highly organised framework of both legislation and mutual recognition of the power on both sides. In fact, to speak of *two* sides seems wrong, since in most cases there is a significant degree of government involvement in the initial coming together of both sides.

The government involvement in the bargaining process is mainly exercised through the Ministry of Social Affairs (Ministerie Van Sociale Zaken), which has considerable legislative powers to impose wage controls, especially in the wider interests of the Dutch economy (in effect, pay restraint). In most cases, however, the Ministry will adopt a position on the sideline, allowing the two sides to bargain within fairly well defined limits.

The right of both unions and employers' associations to come together to resolve basic issues is protected in Dutch law, provided that the representative bodies are officially recognised. This means that on the union side it is one of the three large confederations of unions (one Protestant, one Catholic and the other Non-denominational), and on the employers' side, the Federation of Netherlands Industry (VNO) or one of the three smaller organisations. The confederations on both sides are organised on more or less the same basis, denominational and industry-based, which inevitably makes for better liaison. Most of the detailed bargaining goes on at a company or establishment level, though some national agreements are struck which mainly establish minimum standards or rates, to be improved upon at a disaggregated level.

Of course, many of the potential issues that could cause friction between labour and management are dealt with using the established consultation channels, mainly the works councils. All employing establishments with 100 or more employees must have such a council (this has been the case since 1971) and employers are obliged to consult them on a wide range of issues. In particular, the councils have the power of approval before changes in such basic aspects of work life as pensions, hours of work and holidays can be made, and so these particular issues are unlikely to provide a catalyst to industrial action.

United Kingdom

The atttitude to and control of industrial relations practices in the UK is distinctive in comparison to the other European countries in its degree of freedom. There are few legislative controls either on the conduct of trade unions (though these have increased recently with the 1980 and 1982 Industrial Relations Acts) or on collective bargaining between recognised employee and employer representative groups.

Further differences have already been touched on, e.g. the fragmented structure of the trade union movement, with a combination of craft, industrial and general unions. The organisation of employers is similar, with over 1,000 individual associations, mainly organised on an industry basis (though industry is frequently broadly defined). The corresponding confederations, the TUC for the trade unions and Confederation of British Industry (CBI) for the employers (both public and private industry), though comparatively strong in both membership and influence, are nevertheless not directly involved with collective bargaining, in contrast to the situation in most of the other EEC countries, though not in the USA.

Therefore, most collective bargaining takes place in an unregulated atmosphere, between the relevant union (or unions) and the individual employers' association or company. Bargaining takes place on two levels. At the national level the bargaining tends to concentrate on establishing basic minimum conditions or pay rates, but also provides a framework for further negotiations at a lower level. This lower level usually involves the individual workplace or, in some cases, the company (covering a number of plants), and accounts for the majority of agreements struck. However, in all such cases, the agreements have virtually no legal status and both sides would be free to take industrial action during their course without inhibition. Some agreements do attempt to outline a disputes procedure that should be followed, but this would only tend to preclude official union backing for a strike, with workers still free to take spontaneous action. Since most recorded strikes in the UK are unofficial, increasing such provisions in agreements would have probably little overall effect on the number of stoppages (see Chapter 11).

When collective bargaining breaks down and the result is some form of industrial action, the parties in the dispute have voluntary recourse to the government-sponsored agencies set up to help solve differences. Principally there is the Advisory, Conciliation and Arbitration Service (ACAS), which was established, together with its more formal partner the Central Arbitration Committee (CAC), under the 1975 *Employment Protection Act*. ACAS only provides advice and arranges conciliation or arbitration where necessary, though the decisions may not be accepted by either side. In some cases, use can be made of the Industrial Tribunals (first set up in 1964) which can hear cases from individuals as well as organised groups.

Generally though, the situation in the UK is one where the law is less specific on the conduct of industrial relations. In comparison to the other EEC countries, the UK also appears to differ in its attitude towards the participation of workers in the running of their place of work. Despite the generally favourable overtones of the Bullock Report in 1976, there is still no legal basis for workers' participation or even consultation as exists in most of the other countries.[22]

United States

As in the UK, there is relative freedom in the USA to conduct collective bargaining. The principles of the country's industrial relations system are still greatly dependent on the provisions of the 1935 National Labor Relations Act and subsequent Taft–Hartley Amendments of 1947, which protect the freedom of bargaining.[23] Since then there have been few moves to regulate the conduct of industrial relations.

Bargaining is usually confined to the individual trade unions and the industry employers' associations or company. The unions are strongest in their influence at the local plant level rather than at a national or even state level. The contracts negotiated at this local level can be wide-ranging and can cover issues beyond the usual pay and holidays considerations, for example, matters such as grievance or settlement procedures to be adopted in the event of a dispute. Contracts negotiated and committed usually last for a lengthy period, the norm being three years, and are legally binding on both sides. In addition, the contracts usually contain no-strike (or lockout) clauses, which has an obvious effect on the timing of strike action. For example, in 1980 66.8 per cent of all recorded stoppages beginning in that year occurred during the negotiation of existing agreements, accounting for 89 per cent of all working days lost throughout the year. Strikes are more likely to occur, therefore, when existing agreements are reaching their expiration.

In the event of the two sides in the strike (or lockout) not being able to reach agreement through their own established procedures, there are various channels of help open. The most important is to agree to voluntary arbitration where a mutually acceptable arbitrator is selected to provide a solution. However, the arbitrator's decision is not binding on either side unless such a condition of arbitration before industrial action has been previously in-built into the labour contract. There is no system of compulsory arbitration to settle disputes, though they can be delayed by a special presidentially-sponsored injunction if the stoppage is considered to be potentially damaging to the nation in terms of health or safety, for example.

Overall, therefore, the machinery for resolving disputes is largely left up to free collective bargaining between the two sides. Voluntary assistance is available to the disputants, but only on a request basis and so generally the industrial relations framework remains fairly informal.

Trade unions, industrial relations and strikes

At the beginning of this chapter, it was stated that the issue of the effect of trade union and industrial relations structures on strike activity was a complex one. The examination of the systems in each country given above, albeit relatively superficially, does nothing to counteract this view. It is clear that each of the nine countries has peculiarities which in themselves partly explain the different effects they have on strike activity.

However, there are some similarities which serve to underline the possible impact of such structures on strikes. For example, it is reasonably safe to assume that the density of union membership, at least from a national perspective, is not a reliable guide to strike propensity. For example, if Germany is compared to Italy then it can be seen that though both countries are poles apart in terms of their recorded strike experience, each has a similar level of union density at around 40 per cent (see Table 16.1). Similarly France and the USA, which both have relatively high numbers of working days lost through strikes, each have a low figure of union density at around one quarter of the total labour force.

It may be the case that the type of trade unions in each country will be a more influential factor on strike incidence. Of the nine countries, the UK has the most variegated structure with a some-times unwieldy combination of craft, industrial and general unions, creating their own problems of communication for the employers, let alone the problems of inter-union disputes. This undoubtedly causes difficulties when disputes do occur and perhaps contributes to their duration being longer than would be the case with a more unified structure, as exists in Germany, for example.

In terms of the control of trade unions and their obligations in collective agreements to which they are a party, there are sometimes large differences amongst the nine countries. Again the UK, with the USA and Ireland, have few regulations limiting trade union power, though in the USA, only, contracts agreed through collective bargaining do have legal status. In most of the remaining countries there are stronger commitments to collective agreements, with no-strike (or lockout) clauses being common in France, Germany and the Netherlands, for example. In Italy, though it is common for no-strike clauses to be written into agreements, in practice they are considered legally unenforceable.

More fundamental to the curtailment of strike action must be the facilities that exist on the one hand to prevent disputes developing into stoppages of work, and on the other to bring those disputes that have turned into strikes or lockouts to a resolution quickly. Such facilities will be embodied in the labour law of each country and in the government or quasi-governmental institutions that have been set up to mediate between the two sides.

In the nine countries there is a clearer division on this aspect than all of the others. In those countries which have the most organised and to some extent restrictive set of laws and institutions, such as Denmark and Germany for example, there are also relatively low levels of stoppage activity. Similarly, in those countries where the provision of preventative facilities in particular are few, e.g. Italy, the UK and the USA, the level of strikes is comparatively high. The situation in these countries is not helped by the fact that worker participation in the firm or even consultation on the major employment issues is not as highly developed as in, say, the Belgian, French, German and Dutch works councils, which can by themselves remove many of the catalysts to strike action through the simple provision of information and discussion.

Notes

1. Clegg, H. A., *The System of Industrial Relations in Great Britain* (Oxford Basil Blackwell, 1970).
2. Goodman, J. F. B., 'Trade unions and collective bargaining systems', in Torrington, D. (ed.), *Comparative Industrial Relations in Europe* (London, Associated Business Programmes, 1978), Chapter 3.
3. Batstone, E., Boraston, I. and Frenkel, S., *The Social Organisation of Strikes* (Oxford, Basil Blackwell, 1978), especially Chapter 3.
4. Clegg, H. A., *Trade Unionism under Collective Bargaining* (Oxford, Basil Blackwell, 1976), p. 78.

5. Ibid., p. 71.

6. Kennedy, T., *European Labor Relations* (Lexington, D.C. Heath, 1980), p. 89.

7. The definition of labour force used in each country to determine the denominator for the calculation of union density figures varies. It will depend on the treatment of certain groups by the national trade unions, in particular whether those made unemployed or military personnel are allowed to remain members. In Belgium, for example, the unions also count amongst their members military personnel, the unemployed and certain people over retirement age. If these latter two groups were excluded then union membership density would be considerably higher than the 75 per cent quoted in Table 16.1 and would probably be in the region of 84 per cent.

8. Hanson, C., Jackson, S. and Miller, R., *The Closed Shop* (Aldershot, Gower, 1982), p. 3.

9. The post-entry closed shop is allowed in all but twenty of the fifty states. Employees may only offer to pay union dues as a condition of acceptance.

10. Hanson, C., Jackson, S. and Miller, R., op. cit., p. 8.

11. In the UK some of the professional associations are nevertheless registered with the Certification Office for Trade Unions and Employers' Associations and can be found listed in the *Annual Report of the Certification Officer*.

12. The Bridlington procedure provides that any inter-union disputes must be submitted to TUC conciliation and in the event of an inability by both sides to reach a satisfactory voluntary agreement, then the TUC Disputes Committee can make compulsory decisions. However, the contribution of the inter-union dispute to the total number of strikes has been estimated as being less than 5 per cent. See Jenkins, C. and Sherman, B., *Collective Bargaining* (London, Routledge and Kegan Paul, 1977), p. 36.

13. Clegg, H. A. (1976), op. cit., p. 76.

14. Reported in Industrial Democracy in Europe, International Research Group, *European Industrial Relations* (Oxford, Clarendon Press, 1981), p. 70.

15. Galenson, W., *The Danish System of Labor Relations* (New York, Russell and Russell, 1952), see Chapter 1.

16. Kennedy, T., op. cit., p. 50.

17. This legal requirement is embodied in a 1949 Collective Bargaining Agreement Act, modified in 1952 with a subsequent Act.

18. Kennedy, T., op. cit., p. 180.

19. Industrial Democracy in Europe, op. cit., p. 132.

20. Pollock, H., 'The Irish pattern of industrial relations', *Personnel Management*, Vol. 12:5 (May 1980), pp. 26-9.

21. See ibid., p. 204.

22. The Bullock Report, *Committee of Inquiry on Industrial Democracy* (London, HMSO, 1976).

23. For a lucid discussion of these and subsequent US labour law see Gould, W. B., *A Primer on American Labor Law* (Boston, The MIT Press, 1982).

17 CONCLUSION

To some readers, the structure of this book may seem strange, even ill-conceived, with the first and second parts outlining the sometimes large differences in the measurement, definitions and classifications of stoppages of work statistics, followed by the third part which then goes on to compare the dubious statistics internationally. However, the purpose of this structure is to demonstrate the significant differences that exist and which should be taken into account when using the statistics; there is, therefore, no intended ambivalence.

It is inevitable that if statistics are readily available on a particular subject such as stoppages of work, then they will be used. In this case, the statistics have a good deal of their appeal in international comparisons and this should be encouraged on the whole, provided that they are used with the maximum awareness of the inherent problems. In most cases, however, they are not used in this way and as a result many spurious comparisons are made that can do a great deal of damage to the image of a country. The most familiar example of this is arguably the case of the UK, saddled in recent years with strikes being labelled as 'the British disease', yet every reference to the unadjusted figures shows the UK to be in the middle range of stoppages activity and, given its generally better system of measurement, its position is probably much better than the statistics show.

The foregoing chapters have demonstrated that the differences in the statistical base of each country have not been subjected to great efforts at co-ordination from the supra-national bodies. The ILO guidelines have now been around since 1924 and are both dated and largely ignored by most of the nine countries covered in this study. Thus there exists a series of basically different measurement systems that are largely a reflection of the historical development and perception of strike statistics in each country, such that in Italy and Belgium, the police are still used as the initial focus in the recording system.

There are certain other differences which stand out as being particularly problematic from the point of view of comparability. Foremost amongst these are the different applications of a minimum size threshold for inclusion, and the different treatments of indirect effects and political protest stoppages. Of the nine countries, France is the only one which excludes both indirect effects and political stoppages and such exclusions must make that country's statistics considerable underestimates of the true extent of action. But differences can be found between all countries, such that it can be confidently said that no two countries are compiling their statistics on the same basis.

But even if there were two countries with common characteristics of measurement, it would be fallacious to compare the basic statistics without due regard for the other factors which influence strike propensity in each country. In other words, the statistics as shown are merely reflections of other, more fundamental, factors associated with types of industry and occupations, with, for example, manufacturing and manual workers showing comparatively high strike activity in all nine countries.

However, foremost of the underlying factors which influence strike action must be the effects of trade unions and industrial relations practices. It has been demonstrated that as far as trade unions are concerned, the influence appears to be not so much in the density of membership, but more in the type of union structure to be found. The large industrial unions, characteristic in Continental Europe and the USA, are less prone to the fragmented negotiations often associated with the mixture of craft, general and industrial unions commonly found in the UK and Ireland.

In terms of industrial relations structures, there are similar clear differences in approach, with the more formalised machinery that exists in countries such as Germany and the Netherlands contrasting sharply with the less inhibited atmosphere in, say, the UK or the USA. In many cases, however, the available industrial relations facilities are at work before strike action has started, thus offering the opportunity for conciliation early and pushing the option of a strike far down the long list of steps to take in resolving a dispute. Of course, in many of the countries, the option of strike action is seriously curtailed by the legal status of collective agreements which would make such action illegal, this being the case in most of the countries except the UK and Ireland and possibly Italy, though in Italy it is more by virtue of the fact that the law would probably be unenforceable on this particular point.

Allied to all this is the attitude towards the provision of information to employees and even the involvement of them in the decision-making of the firm. Industrial relations can be greatly eased by the open transmission of basic information to employees, avoiding the suspicion that frequently lies at the root of a dispute. In most of the countries, employee participation has been taken on board, though with varying degrees of vigour and success, and of the nine countries, the UK and the USA are the farthest behind in this, though the realisation of its value in curtailing industrial conflict appears to be there.

All these factors are, therefore, reflected in the statistics of stoppages of work in the nine countries. The most strike-prone countries, according to the best measure of working days lost per 1,000 workers, are generally those countries with the most varied trade union structures, the least formalised industrial relations procedures, and the most flexible labour law: in other words, Italy, Ireland, the UK and the USA. Also, the latter two countries have been relatively slow to adopt worker participation compared to the other countries.

However, it is interesting to note that these four countries, identified as the worst of the nine, are also clearly the best of the nine in terms of their statistical measurement base, as well as the range and depth of coverage of the statistics. In many ways, therefore, an observable high level of stoppage activity will tend to encourage good statistics, which in themselves will be more accurate in showing the true level of activity. By the same token, low recorded levels of activity will tend to subdue interest and may lead to poor measurement. Therefore, it is fair to assume that some of the differences in those countries with high levels of strike activity and those with lower levels, will be attributable to the relative accuracy of the statistics, though this would be impossible to quantify with any precision.

Finally, underlying all the discussion is the basic point that in all of the countries studied, the amount of working time lost due to strikes or lockouts is comparatively small in total, much smaller than say time lost through absence from work. Strikes should, therefore, be seen in proportion to their effect and this should become another factor to consider when pursuing international comparisons of the data.

APPENDIX
DETAILS OF MAIN PUBLICATIONS

This appendix contains brief details of the major publications carrying details of stoppages of work in each country. All the listed publications are readily available and those news or press releases, for example, which may have a restricted circulation have been omitted even though they may be listed as a primary source of information in Part II.

Belgium

1. *Bulletin de Statistique* (Brussels, Institut National de Statistique, monthly). Contains a wide range of statistics on a variety of topics. Information on stoppages of work is usually given each month for the past fourteen months (the latest month being two months earlier than the cover month) and annually for the past six full years.
2. *Annuaire Statistique de la Belgique* (Brussels, Institut National de Statistique, annually). This contains by far the most detailed range of stoppage statistics amongst a wide span of information. The latest information relates to the year prior to the cover year.

Denmark

1. *Nyt Fra Danmarks Statistik—Arbejdsstandsninger* (Copenhagen, Danmarks Statistik, annually). Various newsletters are issued at regular intervals on a wide range of topics. The one covering stoppages of work is issued about the middle of April each year and covers the statistics for the previous full year.
2. *Statistiske Efterretninger* (Copenhagen, Danmarks Statistik, annually). Appears about two months after the newsletter (see above) and more or less confirms the data contained in that.

France

1. *Bulletin Mensuel des Statistiques du Travail* (Paris, Ministère du Travail, monthly). Details of stoppages of work are presented in each month's issue, with the latest information about two months in arrears but going back for at least twelve months.
2. *Supplement au Bulletin Mensuel des Statistique du Travail* (Paris, Ministère du Travail, monthly). The issue providing the most detailed analyses of stoppages appears annually about mid-year and covers the previous full year. For the data up to and including 1980, the details were published on a separate leaflet entitled *Les Conflits du Travail*.

Federal Republic of Germany

1. *Bevölkerung und Erwerbstätigkeit; Reihe 4.3; Streiks und Aussperrungen* (Wiesbaden, Statistisches Bundesamt, annually). This is a special leaflet covering only strikes and lockouts and it appears annually about March, covering the data of the previous full year only.
2. *Arbeits und Sozialstatistik* (Wiesbaden, Statistisches Bundesamt, annually). A compendium of labour and social statistics with good coverage of strikes and lockouts for about a twelve-year period.

Ireland

1. *Irish Statistical Bulletin* (Dublin, Central Statistics Office, quarterly). This publication carries the most comprehensive details of stoppages for the previous full year. The actual quarterly issue carrying the statistics has tended to vary over recent years. For example, in 1980 it was the September issue, while in 1981 it was the December issue.

Italy

1. *Bollettino Mensile di Statistica* (Rome, Istituto Centrale di Statistica, annually). Each monthly issue of this general statistical publication provides brief details of stoppages for the latest thirteen months, about three months in arrears.
2. *Annuario di Statistiche del Lavoro* (Rome, Istituto Centrale di Statistica, annually). A large collection of labour statistics with the most comprehensive statistics on stoppages for the previous five full years, the latest year being the year prior to the cover year.

Netherlands

1. *Sociale Maandstatistiek* (Voorburg, Centraal Bureau voor de Statistiek, monthly). The annual statistics on stoppages appear once a year usually in the May issue and covers the latest full year.

UK

1. *Employment Gazette* (London, Department of Employment/HMSO, monthly). This monthly journal of the DE carries details of stoppages each month with consolidated details for the previous full year appearing in the January issue in a provisional form, followed by a final review in a mid-year issue (June, July or August).
2. *Monthly Digest of Statistics* (London, Central Statistical Office/HMSO, monthly). This contains a brief summary of statistics on disputes for the latest six years (monthly). A more detailed annual summary appears in the *Annual Abstract of Statistics*.

USA

1. *Analysis of Work Stoppages* (Washington DC, US Bureau of Labor Statistics, annually). Until its last issue in 1981, this was the most comprehensive collection of stoppage statistics available in the USA, covering the previous full year with some comparisons with the year before that.
2. *Current Wage Developments* (Washington DC, US Bureau of Labor Statistics, monthly). This is now (from 1982) the major source of statistics on stoppages and details are published each month covering the previous month plus a summary of the basic statistics over a long period.

SELECTED BIBLIOGRAPHY

Aaron, B. (ed.), *Dispute Settlement Procedures in Five Western European Countries* (Los Angeles, Institute of Industrial Relations, University of California, 1969).

Aaron, B. (ed.), *Labour Courts and Grievance Settlement in Western Europe* (Berkeley, University of California Press, 1971).

Aaron, B., 'How other nations deal with emergency disputes', *Monthly Labor Review*, Vol. 95:5 (May 1972).

Andriessen, J. T. M., 'Developments in the Dutch industrial relations system', *Industrial Relations Journal*, Vol. 7:2 (1976).

Ashenfelter, O. and Pencavel, J. H., 'American trade union growth', *Quarterly Journal of Economics*, Vol. 83:3 (August 1969).

Balfour, C., *Industrial Relations in the Common Market* (London, Routledge and Kegan Paul, 1972).

Batstone, E., Boraston, I. and Frenkel, S., *The Social Organisation of Strikes* (Oxford, Basil Blackwell, 1978).

Beyme, K. von, *Trade Unions and Workers Organisations in Industrialised Nations* (London, Sage Publications, 1979).

Blanpain, R., 'Prevention and settlement of collective labour disputes in the EEC countries', *Industrial Law Journal*, Vol. 1:2 and 3 (June and September 1972).

Brown, W. (ed.), *The Changing Contours of British Industrial Relations* (Oxford, Basil Blackwell, 1981).

Clark, O., 'Labour management disputes: a perspective', *British Journal of Industrial Relations*, Vol. 18:1 (March 1980).

Clegg, H. A., *The System of Industrial Relations in Great Britain* (Oxford, Basil Blackwell, 1970).

Clegg, H. A., *Trade Unionism under Collective Bargaining: A Theory based on Comparisons of Six Countries* (Oxford, Basil Blackwell, 1976).

Creigh, S., 'Strikes in OECD countries', *Industrial Relations Journal*, Vol. 13:3 (Autumn 1982).

Creigh, S., Donaldson, N. and Hawthorn, E., 'Stoppage activity in OECD countries', *Employment Gazette*, Vol. 88:11 (November 1980).

Edwards, P. K., 'Size of plant and strike-proneness', *Oxford Bulletin of Economic and Statistics*, Vol. 42:2 (May 1980).

Edwards, P. K., *Strikes in the United States 1881-1974* (Oxford, Basil Blackwell, 1981).

Edwards, P. K., 'The strike-proneness of British manufacturing establishments', *British Journal of Industrial Relations*, Vol. 19:2 (July 1981).

European Foundation for the Improvement of Living and Working Conditions, *The Right to Information in Union Negotiation in Italy* (Rome, Fondazione Brodolini, 1981).

European Industrial Relations Review, 'West German labour court system: a review', *European Industrial Relations Review*, No. 37 (1977).

Evans, E. W. and Creigh, S. W. (eds), *Industrial Conflict in Britain* (London, Frank Cass, 1977).

Fisher, M., *Measurement of Labour Disputes and their Economic Effects* (Paris, OECD, 1973).

Forchheimer, K., 'Some international aspects of the strike movement', *The Bulletin of the Oxford Institute of Economics and Statistics*, Vol. 10 (1948). Reprinted in Evans, E. W. and Creigh, S. W. (eds), *Industrial Conflict in Britain* (London, Frank Cass, 1977), Chapter 10.

Freidman, H. and Meredeen, S., *The Dynamics of Industrial Conflict—Lessons from Ford* (London, Croom Helm, 1980).

Galenson, W., *The Danish System of Labor Relations* (New York, Russell and Russell, 1952).

Gennard, J., 'The financial costs and returns of strikes', *British Journal of Industrial Relations*, Vol. 20:2 (July 1982).

Givry, J. de, 'Labour courts as channels for the settlement of labour disputes', *British Journal of Industrial Relations*, Vol. 6:3 (November 1968).

Hanson, C., Jackson, S. and Miller, D., *The Closed Shop* (Aldershot, Gower, 1982).

Harrison, R., *Worker's Participation in Western Europe* (London, Institute of Personnel Management, 1976).

Hoffman, E. B., *Resolving Labor-Management Disputes: A Nine Country Comparison* (New York, Conference Board, 1973).

Hunter, L. C., 'Dispute trends and the shape of strikes to come', *Personnel Management*, Vol. 12:10 (October 1980).

Hyman, R., *Strikes* (London, Collins/Fontana 1972).

Ingham, G. K., *Strikes and Industrial Conflict, Britain and Scandinavia* (London, Macmillan, 1974).

International Labour Office, *Conciliation in Industrial Disputes,* (Geneva, ILO, 1973).

International Labour Office, *International Recommendations on Labour Statistics* (Geneva, ILO, 1976).

International Labour Office, *Conciliation and Arbitration Procedures in Labour Disputes* (Geneva, ILO, 1980).

Jackson, M. P., *Industrial Relations* (London, Croom Helm, 1972).

Kahn-Freund, O. and Hepple, B., *Laws against Strikes—International Comparisons in Social Policy* (London, Fabian Society, Research Series 305, 1972).

Kassalow, E., *Trade Unions and Industrial Relations: An International Comparison* (New York, Random House, 1969).

Kaufman, B. E., 'The determinants of strikes in the United States, 1900-1977', *Industrial and Labor Relations Review*, Vol. 35:4 (July 1982).

Kendall, W., *The Labour Movement in Europe* (London, Allen Lane, 1975).

Kennedy, T., *European Labor Relations* (Lexington, D. C. Heath, 1980).

Kerr, C. and Siegel, A., 'The inter-industry propensity to strike—an international comparison'. From Kornhauser, A., Dubin, R. and Ross, A. M. (eds.), *Industrial Conflict* (New York, MacGraw-Hill, 1954) and reprinted in Evans, E. W. and Creigh, S. W. (eds), *Industrial Conflict in Britain* (London, Frank Cass, 1977), Chapter 11.

Knowles, K. G. J. C., *Strikes—A study in Industrial Conflict* (Oxford, Basil Blackwell, 1952).

Kornhauser, A., Dubin, R. and Ross, A. M. (eds), *Industrial Conflict* (New York, McGraw-Hill, 1954).

Korpi, W., 'Unofficial strikes in Sweden', *British Journal of Industrial Relations*, Vol. 19:1 (March 1981).

Lewis, P. E. T. and Makepeace, G. H., 'The measurement of workers' militancy over time', *Bulletin of Economic Research*, Vol. 32:2 (November 1980).

McCarthy, W. E. J., 'The nature of Britain's strike problem', *British Journal of Industrial Relations*, Vol. 8 (1970).

McCarthy, W. E. J., 'The reasons given for striking', *Bulletin of the Oxford University Institute of Economics and Statistics*, Vol. 21 (1959).

Müller-Jentsch, W., 'Strikes and strike trends in West Germany, 1950-78', *Industrial Relations Journal*, Vol. 12:4 (July/August 1981).

Mulvey, C., 'Unemployment and the incidence of strikes in the Republic of Ireland 1942-66', *Journal of Economic Studies*, Vol. 3 (1968).

Organisation for Economic Co-operation and Development, *Collective Bargaining and Government Policies in Ten OECD Countries* (Paris, OECD, 1979).

Organisation for Economic Co-operation and Development, *Labour Disputes: A Perspective* (Paris, OECD, 1979).

Owen Smith, E., *Trade Unions in the Developed Countries* (London, Croom Helm, 1981).

Oxnam, D. W., 'International comparisons of industrial conflict: an appraisal', *Journal of Industrial Relations*, Vol. 7 (July 1965).

Oxnam, D. W., 'Issues in industrial conflict: an international comparison', *Journal of Industrial Relations*, Vol. 13 (June 1971).

Paldam, M. and Pederson, P. J., 'The macro-economic strike model: a study of seventeen countries, 1948-1975', *Industrial and Labor Relations Review*, Vol. 35:4 (July 1982).

Pencavel, J. H., 'An investigation into industrial strike activity in Britain', *Economica*, Vol. 37 (1970).

Pollock, H., *Industrial Relations in Practice* (Dublin, O'Brien Press, 1982).

Pollock, H., 'The Irish pattern of industrial relations', *Personnel Management*, Vol. 12:5 (May 1980).

Rimlinger, G. V., 'International differences in the strike propensity of coal miners: experience in four countries', *Industrial and Labor Relations Review*, Vol. 13 (1959).

Ross, A. M. and Hartman, P. T., *Changing Patterns of Industrial Conflict* (New York, Wiley, 1960).

Schregle, J., 'Comparative industrial relations: pitfalls and potential', *International Labour Review*, Vol. 120:1 (January/February 1981).

Shalev, H., 'Lies, damned lies and strike statistics'. In Crouch, C. and Pizzorno, A.,

The Resurgence of Class Conflict in Western Europe Since 1978, Vol. 1 (London, Macmillan, 1980).

Shorey, J., 'An Inter-industry analysis of strike frequency', *Economica*, Vol. 43 (November 1976).

Shorey, J., 'The size of the work unit and strike incidence', *Journal of Industrial Economics*, Vol. 23 (1975).

Shorter, E. and Tilly, C., *Strikes in France 1830-1968* (Cambridge, Cambridge University Press, 1974).

Silver, M., 'Recent British strike trends: a factual analysis', *British Journal of Industrial Relations*, Vol. 11 (1973).

Smith, C. T. B., Clifton, R., Makeham, P., Creigh, S. W. and Burn, R. V., *Strikes in Britain*, DE Manpower Paper No. 15 (London, HMSO, 1978).

Sorge, A., 'The evolution of industrial democracy in the countries of the European Community', *British Journal of Industrial Relations*, Vol. 14 (1976).

Sorge, A. and Warner, M., 'The context of industrial relations in GB and West Germany', *Industrial Relations Journal*, Vol. 11 (March/April 1980), pp. 44-9.

Stieber, J., 'Unauthorised strikes under the American and British industrial relations systems', *British Journal of Industrial Relations*, Vol. 6 (1968).

Sweet, T. G. and Jackson, D. *The Classification and Interpretation of Strike Statistics: An International Comparative Analysis*, Working Paper No. 97 (Birmingham, University of Aston Management Centre, 1978).

Torrington, D. (ed.), *Comparative Industrial Relations in Europe* (London, Associated Business Programmes, 1978).

Turner, H. A., *Is Britain Really Strike-Prone?* (Cambridge, Cambridge University Press, 1969).

Turner, H. A., Clack, G. and Roberts, G., *Labour Relations in the Motor Industry* (Cambridge, Cambridge University Press, 1967).

Walsh, K., 'An analysis of strikes in four EEC countries', *Industrial Relations Journal*, Vol. 13:4 (Winter 1982).

Walsh, K., 'Industrial disputes activity in some EEC countries: a regional perspective', *Manpower Studies*, No. 3 (Autumn 1981).

Walsh, K., *Industrial Disputes—Methods and Measurement in the European Community* (Luxembourg, EUROSTAT, 1982).

Windmuller, J., *Labor Relations in the Netherlands* (Ithaca, Cornell University Press, 1969).

INDEX